Using discounted cash flow in investment appraisal
Third Edition

M. G. Wright, BCom, FCCA, FCIS

McGRAW-HILL BOOK COMPANY

London · New York · St Louis · San Francisco · Auckland · Bogotá
Guatemala · Hamburg · Lisbon · Madrid · Mexico · Montreal
New Delhi · Panama · Paris · San Juan · São Paulo · Singapore
Sydney · Tokyo · Toronto

Published by

McGRAW-HILL Book Company (UK) Limited

Shoppenhangers Road
Maidenhead, Berkshire, England SL6 2QL
Telephone Maidenhead (0628) 23432
Fax 0628 35895

British Library Cataloguing in Publication Data

Wright, M. G. (Maurice Gordon)
   Using discounted cash flow in investment appraisal.–3rd ed.
   1. Capital investment by business firms. Decision making. Discounted
     cash flow techniques
   I. Title   II. Wright, M. G. (Maurice Gordon). Discounted cash flow
   658.1'52

   ISBN 0–07–707327–4

Library of Congress Cataloging-in-Publication Data

Wright, M. G. (Maurice Gordon)
   Using discounted cash flow in investment appraisal/M. G. Wright.
   –3rd ed.
   p. cm.
   Rev. ed. of: Discounted cash flow. 2nd ed. [1973]
   ISBN 0–07–707327–4
   1. Capital investments—Evaluation. 2. Discounted cash flow.
   I. Wright, M. G. (Maurice Gordon). Discounted cash flow.
   II. Title.
   HG4028.C4W75   1990
   658.15'2–dc20   89–13308

12345IP   92310

Typeset by Burgess & Son (Abingdon) Ltd.
Printed in Great Britain at the University Press, Cambridge

Using discounted cash flow in investment appraisal

Third Edition

LEEDS METROPOLITAN UNIVERSITY

Calverley Street Library
∼eds LS1 3HE

ᴐtʰ ¹   te ʒʰ⌐

To my parents

Contents

Appendices

48-102
178,129&126

Preface

This book is primarily concerned with how a capital budgeting system should work within the managerial framework, and will be looked at more from the practitioner's point of view, whether he or she be a manager making decisions or someone concerned with the preparation of the data on which such decisions are made, rather than dealing in depth with the theoretical concepts on which discounted cash flow is based. Basic concepts cannot be ignored as many people may become involved in investment appraisal who do not have the necessary understanding of those concepts. It is necessary that all involved in the appraisal system have an understanding of the basis of DCF and the meaning of the DCF or internal rate of return, and this aspect is dealt with at the beginning of the book. However, perhaps the most critical aspect of introducing a formal investment appraisal system based upon cash flows is the problem of measuring the cash flows themselves. Any investment appraisal system adopted will only be as good as the information that is fed into the appraisal process, therefore unless the preparation of this data is based upon sound principles and carried out in a competent way, the outcome of the appraisal process will itself be flawed.

The focus of the book is therefore aimed at helping those who will be involved in formulating investment proposals, in assessing the planned operations of the project concerned and the ensuing cash flows, and in the decision-making process based upon the evaluation of individual projects, a process that will at the end of the day produce the overall investment programme for the business. The process of identifying areas for new investment and the planning of how those investments will be made are the essential requirements for a successful capital budgeting system. The appraisal techniques that are used to make selections from those projects identified as being useful are purely mechanical. Once the cash flows for an investment project have been determined, then whatever method of appraisal that may have been chosen can be applied to those cash flows through the medium of a computer program or clerical work.

The managerial aspects of investment decisions are stressed because there is always a danger that management may think that once an appraisal method has been adopted, then it has discharged its responsibilities for the appraisal process. This is, of course, far from the truth. There are many decisions that must be taken by top management to set the parameters within which the appraisal system should function. Such matters as identifying strategic areas for investment, the minimum acceptable rate of return, target levels of profitability, required balance within the totality of new investment, etc., these are critical decisions that management should make and constantly keep under review. Above all there is the need for management to specify the focus for the future of the business so that there are known areas in which investment has to be made, rather than leaving the formulation of new investment to line managers who are likely to follow their own perception of what new investment is required.

Section 1

Basic techniques

1. *Capital investment appraisal and profitability*

As implied by the title, this book is concerned with the meaning and use of discounted cash flow (DCF) and, in particular, how management should use the technique. As a technique, however, it is purely mechanistic and it would be quite unrealistic to deal with the technique without first looking at how it fits into the general management processes, and in particular the role that it plays in the critical process of allocating funds to specific uses within a business. Management's success or failure in this process will have a major impact on the long-term future of the business.

Concentration on mathematical management techniques often appears to endow them with decision-making qualities which quite frequently they do not possess. This applies particularly to DCF. Unless management plays its proper role in setting the parameters within which the technique must operate and carries out its role in identifying investment opportunities, wrong decisions may be taken which may then be blamed on the technique. Before looking at the technique it is essential that one should look first of all at the overall management system, and at financial planning and control areas as they affect investment decisions.

Profitability and growth

The principal objective of any business in the private sector should be the *long-term* maximization of the owner's interests. This can only be achieved through proper planning and control of profitability and it is by that criterion that management will be judged. Profitability is a wider concept than profit. It relates the latter to the resources that have to be invested to earn that profit and it is this that makes it a key measure of the efficiency of the management team.

Profitability is such a key issue because it has a decisive impact upon the future growth prospects of the business. A company with a low level of profitability will generate little profit compared with similar businesses and, therefore, investors will see little merit in that company as an investment and will be unwilling to invest in it. Lenders will also be reluctant to lend, since there will be a lower cover for debt service. As a consequence the company will find it difficult or impossible to raise funds for expansion, in addition of course to the low level of funds generated internally.

On the other hand a company with a high level of profitability will be generating a large flow of funds which can be ploughed back into the business and used to pay higher returns to investors. The greater security will make it easier to borrow money if necessary. Overall it will be perceived as an attractive investment to both equity investors and lenders. In the public sector it is increasingly recognized that the economic use of resources in the provision of services and the profitability of enterprises are critical factors for judging the effectiveness of the managements of the service or enterprise on both efficiency and political grounds.

The profitability of a business is of importance to a much wider community than those who work or invest in it. The economic health of the country as a whole will rely on having numerous profitable enterprises within its borders. No advanced country today can avoid the problem of providing social services for the poorer sections of the community, and for providing internal and external security. These are going to absorb some of the country's resources and it is what is left that is available for personal consumption and new capital formation. The higher the general level of profitability in the country the easier it will be to provide those essential services while at the same time providing better opportunities for growth.

QUALITY OF INVESTMENT

Commentators and politicians in the United Kingdom have since the Second World War continually urged industrialists to invest ever greater amounts in productive facilities, and indeed have often provided major tax incentives to achieve that. In this concentration on the *volume* of investment, the *quality* of investment has sometimes been overlooked. Artificially making projects profitable through tax incentives and grants is no substitute for a situation which is conducive to fundamentally sound, i.e. profitable, investments.

If £5 million is invested in a sophisticated plant to make, say, shoes, and that plant does nothing more than break even, then the investment of that money and the underlying resources that have been used contribute nothing to the resources of the firm or of the country. However, a similar investment that yields a profit before tax of 20 per cent on the capital invested contributes to corporate growth, and through taxation, contributes to the national well-being. There should, therefore, be no conflict between the national interest and that of the firm. Indeed, the former will be reinforced if it is based upon a large number of profitable enterprises. This will be true irrespective of the political system under which the country functions.

LONG-TERM NATURE OF INVESTMENT DECISIONS

As already stated, management's decisions on how the business's resources are allocated to specific uses profoundly affect profitability. The management that looks ahead, that is innovative and establishes a sound method of selecting investment projects will be one that is successful. Investment projects often lock up substantial parts of a company's resources for long

4

periods of time. Investment in a highly automated plant cannot be reversed quickly. Funds will remain locked up in that use until they are recouped through the generation of cash flows from that project, together with the added profit, or the project is scrapped.

It is this long-term characteristic that distinguishes the investment decision from many other business decisions. Setting the wrong stock levels or allowing customers to take too long to pay their accounts are mistakes that can be remedied in the relatively short term, the timescale being determined by factors such as the length of time it takes to absorb or sell surplus stock, or to collect customers' accounts. The timespan for correcting wrong investment decisions will, however, be the normal working life of the plant unless the firm decides to write off the funds as having been effectively lost.

It is not only funds invested in *fixed tangible* assets that will be locked up by the wrong investment decisions. The investment in fixed assets will, in many cases, need to be backed up by investment in working capital, through increases in stocks and debtors. The investment decision, therefore, influences the totality of funds employed in the business and the return that will be earned on them.

Each year a firm will have a finite sum of funds available for investment—the amount available being dependent in many ways on the success of management. Each commitment of those funds to an unprofitable use decreases the amount available for future profitable investments. It follows, therefore, that the way in which a business allocates the resources at its disposal will have a far-reaching effect on its long-term profitability. The decision processes by which funds are allocated, the criteria used for the selection of projects and management's role at each stage are the crucial elements for success.

Allocation as a two-stage process

A view widely held—if not practised—is that *all* decision-making in a business starts with long-term planning or corporate strategy, that if management has not looked at the future and decided how it will respond to changes in the marketplace, technology, etc., it cannot make rational short-term decisions. This does not mean to say that relative profitability does not have a major role to play in the process of funds allocation. What it does recognize is that selection in terms of relative profitability should only take place within areas where management has decided there is a long-term requirement so that new investment focuses on the long-term needs of the business. It is top management's task to ensure the long-term viability of the business and this will only be done by maximizing long-term profitability rather than simply looking at the short term. Without the long-term view investment proposals will tend to be initiated by line managers who may be pursuing quite worthy objectives from their own, more limited, point of view. These objectives may not, however, be those that are required for the business as an entity.

This requirement for long-term profitability indicates that there should be two levels of decision-making in this area:

1. *Primary allocation.* This primary allocation should be made at board of director or equivalent level in general terms, through the setting of long-term plans for the business. This should ensure that the right balance of investments are made to meet the long-term requirements of the business.

2. *Project selection.* This stage operates within the strategic framework outlined above. It comprises the continuing process of formulating new investment proposals, appraisal by profitability and selection by management.

This process can be compared with the function of the chiefs of staff of the armed forces in time of war. They set out the general objectives to be pursued in each theatre of operations, and allocate the resources at their disposal in such a way as to maximize the possibility of bringing the war to a successful conclusion. Within the resources allocated to him, each theatre commander attempts to formulate operations designed to achieve the objectives the chiefs of staff have set him, and obtain approval for such operations to be mounted. This allocation of resources and approval of individual operations is the method by which the chiefs of staff ensure that the war effort as a whole pursues the defined objectives, and that each theatre commander does not fight his own private war without regard to the balance of the war effort as a whole. Naturally there will be consultation and discussion at all levels of command, but the thrust of the war effort can only be achieved by policy-making and resources allocation at the top.

The military scene has a message for management. Policy decisions cannot be left to line managers who would then each pursue what he or she perceived as the required goals. Policy-making should always be under the control and direction of the board of directors whose prime responsibility should be to give the business its sense of purpose and stimulus.

CORPORATE STRATEGY

This policy-making process is today usually formalized under the title of *corporate strategy* or *long-term planning*. This should be the starting point for all decision-making in an organization. It comprises the definition of the objectives of the business, how they are to be achieved, and the resources that will be required.

This process of formulating a corporate strategy can be summarized as follows:

1. *Definition of objectives.* It can be argued that all commercially orientated organizations have the same principal objective—to make a profit. Other

objectives such as 'to be the technological leader', or 'to achieve a stated market share', will, if they lead to an unsatisfactory level of profits, be revised. They are in effect subject to the test of profitability. What is an *acceptable* level of profit will at the end of the day depend on the overall level of return that it would offer to investors. The measurement of this acceptable level of profit will depend on management decisions about how the finance for the business is to be raised.

2. *The strategy*. Having defined the level of profit needed to make the company viable in the long term, management must then make decisions about *how* it is going to achieve that level of profit. It will make an appraisal of the strengths and weaknesses of the business, how the environment is likely to change within the planning horizon, and how the business can best exploit those changes.

Such a process will determine factors such as the human skills required and how the organization is going to develop. Thus if one is drawing up a management development programme one can only logically do so when the skills required and the way the organization is going to develop have been defined. It will outline where new investment is required over the planning period. By this process it has set the framework within which the capital budgeting process must operate, and by defining required levels of profitability has established criteria by which new investment must be judged.

OTHER CONSIDERATIONS IN PROJECT APPRAISAL

Profitability is, of course, only one of the criteria incorporated into a coherent, balanced, management strategy. If all of the projects undertaken were ones which produce little profits in the early years and large ones in the later years, the company might experience considerable difficulties in those early years. While it is often stated that investors look too much at short-term returns and too little at the long term, it has to be recognized that the perception of the company in the investor community would suffer during that period of low profitability and that this would be reflected in the company's share price. The overall task of management is to prepare a *balanced* basket of projects which provide a consistent pattern of profits over time. Only where there is a very close relationship between management and shareholders in which the long-term aspect can be properly put over is it likely that a period of low profits would be accepted, even if that would produce, after a few years, a better return.

The further away in time that an event occurs the greater the risk. All investment decisions are looking into the future and the future is never certain. Aspects of uncertainty and risk are ones which are germane to any investment decision and these will be dealt with as a separate issue later on.

The need to have a coherent long-term strategy for the investment of funds has been stressed at some length. If the allocation process is left to line managers each will put forward what he or she sees as their most important requirement. Without a strategy such managers may be unable to weigh up the merits of their investment proposals as compared with those of other managers, since each will be pursuing his or her own particular set of objectives. Moreover, their horizon tends to be restricted to the immediate environment within which they operate, and this may be a relatively small segment of the business.

The only way to achieve a coherent balance of new investment is by making known the corporate strategy to all concerned and ensuring that the pattern of investment needed to achieve the defined objectives is adhered to. Without this discipline it would be a little bit like driving a motor car with the windscreen painted over—one would only see what is on either side and behind. The most important direction—in front—would be obscured.

MINIMUM PROFITABILITY CRITERION

The key importance of the investment decision can be seen if one sets it within the context of the cash flows of a business as shown in Figure 1.1. A business derives the cash that it needs to survive and to grow from:

1. funds provided by the owners of the business, in the case of companies from share capital;
2. money borrowed by the business;
3. the cash generated by the business and retained within it, that is to say the difference between the sales value and those expenses involving cash flows. What is retained is that value after payments out of profits of dividends, etc.

Each of these sources contributes to a 'pool' of funds which represents the resources that management has available to use in the business.

This pool of funds has a cost. That cost is evident in the case of money that has been borrowed, since the rate of interest will be clearly defined. However, the cost of funds provided by the owners of the business, whether the original capital or profits and gains left in the business, is more difficult to define. In the case of preference shares the rate of dividend is stated, but in the case of equity some measure of opportunity cost is more appropriate, i.e. what the shareholder could earn on those funds if they were at his disposal to invest. This concept is dealt with in detail on page 157.

Figure 1.1 shows quite clearly the critical nature of the capital investment decision. It stands at the interface between the decision area relating to how funds are raised, and the decision area concerned with how those funds are to be deployed within the business to earn a profit. One aim of this investment decision should be to ensure that as far as possible the uses to which

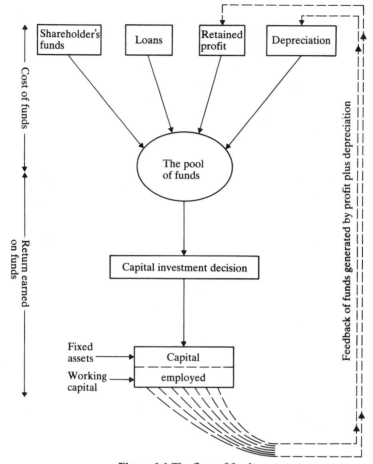

Figure 1.1 The flow of funds

management put the funds earn a return that more than covers the cost of the 'pool' of funds. If the average after-tax cost of money is 10 per cent, there is no merit in using that money on projects which earn only 8 per cent.

The decision is a critical one in that if management is good at identifying investment opportunities—which is the concern of corporate strategy—and if it is good at selecting projects—which is the function of investment appraisal techniques—and if it is good at managing those projects selected, the business will have a strong cash flow, profits and therefore dividends will be high, and the business will find it easy to raise capital to finance growth. If, on the other hand, it is bad at these things, then cash flow will be poor, profits low or non-existent, and it will be difficult or impossible to raise new capital to finance growth.

Selection of projects

When management has made the strategic decisions about the required pattern of new investment there is then the problem of how the day-to-day investment decisions are to be made within that overall strategic framework. It is this stage, based upon the selection and evaluation of projects, with which this book is primarily concerned. In particular the book will be dealing with one method of capital investment appraisal, that known as *discounted cash flow* (DCF).

The requirement of any method of selecting projects is that it should enable management to make comparisons of the profitability of the projects available. Each project requires the use of part of the firms's capital for varying periods of time and should earn a return that covers the cost of the capital that it uses, and provide for an element of profit. Any appraisal system that is adopted should, therefore, enable investment projects to be measured against two criteria:

1. to ensure that, out of any given series of investment proposals, the ones with the higher rates of return will be chosen, and those with lower returns rejected, subject to the need for a balanced portfolio of activities mentioned earlier;
2. to ensure, as far as possible, that investments are not made in projects that give a rate of return lower than the cost of capital.

Few businesses will have enough funds available to be able to invest in every project presented for approval which meet criterion 2 above. Management, therefore, should adopt a selection method that enables it to rank projects in order of profitability so that the relative desirability of each of them in terms of profitability can be readily seen.

The second criterion requires a comparison between the rate of return that can be earned on the project and the average cost of funds to the business. Although each business has a limit to the amount of funds available, that limit may be wide enough for some businesses to be able to invest in projects giving a rate of return lower than the cost of capital. Where this arises, management must set a 'cut-off' or criterion rate of return that will be the minimum acceptable rate of return for any project.

This cut-off rate will be closely related to the cost of capital but may be adjusted for a number of factors, including an allowance for the degree of uncertainty embodied in the estimated rates of return for projects, and for the investment of some of the funds in projects that are essential for the future of the business but give no rate of return. Where there are insufficient projects that meet that criterion rate, i.e. there are more funds available than acceptable investments, management should look at its long-term strategy and decide whether those surplus funds should be carried forward to future years, or whether they should be distributed to the owners of the business.

As stated above it may be that some investment projects may be essential but have no rate of return and are not subject to the criteria discussed. Some funds may have to be invested in order that the business can continue to be carried on, yet produce no profit at all. For example, a local authority may require the modernization of toilet facilities or the provision of adequate car-parking facilities. The Health and Safety Inspectorate may lay down conditions under which employees must work, and so on. Such investments must be made without recourse to the usual criteria. Similarly, some projects, such as the provision of recreational and canteen facilities, while desirable, may not be susceptible to assessment by the normal means.

TYPES OF PROBLEM

Investment of funds within a business may fall within a number of different areas, each of which requires a different approach to finding a solution. These types of investment and how to tackle their solution are shown in Table 1.1.

Table 1.1 Types of investment problem

1. *Expansion*	Whether to build and equip a new factory or expand.	The investment is the amount that will be locked up by such an expansion. Against this will be measured the additional profits that are expected to flow from that expansion.
2. *Replacement and modernization*	Replacement of existing plant by more efficient plant.	The return on this investment is the saving in costs that is expected to flow from the use of more efficient plant.
3. *Choice problems*	In 1 and 2 above there may be more than one way of achieving the required result. Which method is best?	Alternative methods must be ranked in order of profitability so that one can select the most profitable.
4. *Lease or buy*	To purchase outright or lease plant.	Where a decision has been made to go ahead with a project there is a further decision to be made. Purchase requires the outlay of cash. Will the benefits of ownership rather than leasing give a large enough return?
5. *Financing problems*	Whether to redeem fixed return sources of finance.	Refunding operations involve costs and perhaps a premium on nominal values. This can then be compared with interest and other outlays that are saved as a result.

EVALUATION OF INVESTMENT PROBLEMS

The common features of all of the types of problem outlined above are that an outlay of cash is required at the beginning of the project, and that this will be followed by greater incoming cash flows in following years. The solution to the problems involve evaluating in some way the value of that series of incoming cash flows against the initial outlay. The problems are not, of course, new ones. They have been present ever since man first accumulated capital and then faced the dilemma of what to do with it. In many cases the investment of that capital has been an intuitive process or has accorded with some need to fulfil some personal ambition.

Modern business is, however, a complex activity. The personal vision or intuition has given ground to the need for more scientific methods of management by groups of people. Decisions, including the investment decision, are taken by and affect more than one person, and this requires some discipline in the methods that are used. Not only are more logical methods of reaching decisions required, but also they should conform to a pattern which enables the results of those decisions to be understood by all those people that are affected by them.

Methods of investment evaluation have progressed as the techniques of management have progressed. Perhaps the technique most widely used in the past is the *accounting rate of return* based on the conventional concept of profit. This was felt to be inadequate and the use of *pay back period* was introduced. It may be instructive to look at the deficiencies of both of these methods before examining DCF to see why the search for better methods has continued.

Accounting rate of return method

This method employs conventional accounting and budgeting techniques to assess the increase in annual profits that is expected to accrue from a new investment, and then compares this amount with the capital that will have to be invested in the project. The measurement of incremental revenues and costs results from the planning associated with the project in the same way as annual budgets are based on plans for the business as a whole for the ensuing year. The process should therefore be readily understood by all those associated with budgets and accounts. The increased returns are recorded in the accounting period of the business in which the profits are normally recorded and does not take into account the timing of these periods.

Let us assume that the directors of X plc are considering the investment of £100,000 in a new packing machine. An investigation would be made into the cost and other benefits that would accrue from that investment. Let us assume that these changes would add £15,000 to annual profits after deprecia-

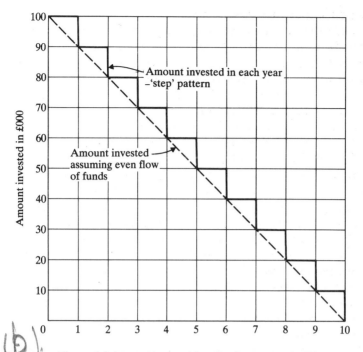

Figure 1.2 Amount invested in a fixed asset over its life

tion and before tax. The accounting rate of return for this project would then be measured as the additional annual profit of £15,000 as a percentage of the amount that would have to be invested. In the example given the percentage rate of return would be 15,000 × 100/100,000 = 15 per cent.

This measurement seems to be quite logical, but does it take into account all of the factors? For example, the percentage return has been calculated on the original investment. If, however, we assume that the machine is depreciated by equal amounts each year over, say, its ten year life, then in accounting terms the investment will be decreased by one tenth of the original amount each year. This decrease in the investment is shown in Figure 1.2. At the end of the first year the investment is reduced to £90,000, at the end of the second year to £80,000, and so on, until at the end of the tenth year its value is reduced to zero. If we were to assume that cash flows accrued evenly over time on the same basis, then the amount of investment locked up in the project at any one time would be that shown by the dotted line.

It can be seen from Figure 1.2 that the *average* amount invested over the whole life of the machine is of the order of £50,000. The accounting rate of return on this basis would be 15,000 × 100/50,000 = 30 per cent.

Another factor which might be considered is taxation. Both the calcula-

13

tions used so far are on a 'before-tax' basis. They could, however, be calculated on an 'after-tax' basis. Assuming that the effective tax rate is 35 per cent, then the annual profits after tax would be £9,750, and the accounting rates of return would be 9.75 per cent on the original investment and 19.5 per cent on the average investment basis.

DEFICIENCIES OF THE ACCOUNTING RATE OF RETURN

The problem posed by the various methods by which one can calculate the accounting rate of return could be overcome by adopting a common basis for calculating both the amount of investment required, and the increment in annual profits. There are, however, more serious objections to the use of this method.

If all investment projects had the same length of life and profits accrued evenly over the life of the project, then this method might well provide an acceptable basis for the selection of projects. In real life, of course, this is not the case. Projects will have wide variations in expected lives, and profits may accrue unevenly over that life. Both of these factors will affect the real rate of return because this method of selection does not take into account timing differences.

To illustrate this timing factor and its impact on the project selection process, let us assume that management is presented with three projects and only has the funds available to select one. The amount that would have to be invested in each of the projects, and the estimated pattern of profits, are shown in Table 1.2. The accounting rate of return shows that each of these projects is equally profitable whatever basis of measurement is used. On this assessment management would be indifferent in choosing between the three projects. But can it really be said that these three projects are equally profitable?

Comparing Project A with Project B it can be seen that profits arising from Project B come much earlier in the life of the project than those from Project A. The funds released by the earlier accrual of profits can be put to work to earn more profits through investment in other projects and, because of that earning power, are more valuable to the business than profits arising in later periods of time. In other words there is a *time differential* in the earnings of these two projects that must be allowed for when ranking them in order of profitability. The accounting rate of return has not taken into account the effect of that time differential. Management should clearly prefer Project B to Project A.

In Project C another area of difficulty is encountered. It has a longer life than either of the other projects, although the accounting rate of return shows that it is equally profitable. How can we incorporate the effect that this extra year's earnings will have on the rate of return in the assessment of the project? This is impossible to do without the use of more sophisticated

Table 1.2 Comparison of three projects by the accounting rate of return method

	Project A	Project B	Project C
Amount of investment	£10,000	£10,000	£10,000
Increase in profit (after depreciation)	£	£	£
Year 1	200	2,300	1,500
Year 2	1,500	2,000	1,500
Year 3	1,500	1,500	1,500
Year 4	2,000	1,500	1,500
Year 5	2,300	200	1,500
Year 6	—	—	1,500
Total profits	7,500	7,500	9,000
Life of project	5 years	5 years	6 years
Average annual increase in profits	£1,500	£1,500	£1,500
Rate of return:			
On original investment	15%	15%	15%
On average sum invested	30%	30%	30%

techniques since it requires one to weigh up the relevant time advantages of the higher returns of Project B in years 1 and 2 against the higher returns of Project C in years 4, 5 and 6. What is needed is a system that will take into account both the timing and life differences of a series of investment proposals, and will incorporate the effect of these in the rate of return.

Pay back period

In order to avoid some of the pitfalls that we have seen in the accounting rate of return method, and recognizing that the speed of recoupment of the original capital investment in a project may be an important element in its appraisal, a further method was evolved, known as the *pay back period*. The basis for the decision using this method is the length of time it takes to recoup the investment made in the project.

Since this method is concerned with the speed of recoupment of the investment, it must be based on *cash flow* rather than profit, since one cannot say that the investment has been recouped until the cash has been received. This concept of cash flow will be more fully dealt with on page 48, but essentially it is a measure of the amount of cash that will be released from the project, and therefore free for investment elsewhere, and can be defined as the difference between the cash generated from extra sales etc., or cost savings, and those extra expenses involving cash outlays. In accounting terms this could be expressed as the additional profit plus depreciation, adjusted for any extra tax payments involved.

When used in this way the pay back method requires the accumulation of the cash flows, year by year, until they equal the amount of the original investment. The length of time required to do this is the pay back period for the project. The basis for making the investment decision is then to select those projects with the shortest pay back periods.

To illustrate the process assume that the directors of AB plc are considering investing the sum of £10,000 in additional machinery. The extra cash flows that are expected to arise are shown in the second column of Table 1.3.

At the end of the first year's life the company will have recouped £1,000 of its original investment; by the end of the second year £2,200, and so on, until at the end of the fifth year the whole of the original investment of £10,000 has been recouped. In the example given the project would be said to have a five-year pay back period.

Table 1.3 Calculation of the pay back period

Amount investment in the project £10,000

Cash flows:

Year	Annual £	Cumulative £
1	1,000	1,000
2	1,200	2,200
3	2,000	4,200
4	3,000	7,200
5	2,800	10,000

Pay back period: five years

It should be noted that the method makes no attempt to measure profitability. All that it provides is the length of time that it takes to recoup the amount invested in the project, the assumption being that projects with a short pay back period are better investments than those with long pay back periods. However, it does not in any way take into account cash flows that arise *after* the pay back period.

Consider the case where management has to choose between two projects, A and B. Each project requires £10,000 to be invested, and the annual cash flows are those shown in Table 1.4. Project A has an anticipated life of four years and Project B one of ten years.

Project A has a pay back of four years, which coincides with the termination of the project, there being no further cash flows. Project B has a pay

Table 1.4 Comparison of two projects by the pay back method

	Project A £10,000			Project B £10,000	
Investment:					
Cash flows:					
Year	Annual £	Cumulative £		Annual £	Cumulative £
1	2,000	2,000		1,000	1,000
2	3,000	5,000		1,200	2,200
3	3,000	8,000		1,500	3,700
4	2,000	10,000		2,000	5,700
5				2,300	8,000
6				1,800	9,800
7				1,800	11,600
8				1,800	13,400
9				1,700	15,100
10				1,000	16,100
Pay back period:	4 years			$6\frac{1}{9}$ years	

back of just over six years, but its cash flow continues beyond that period for nearly another four years. Using the pay back criterion management would opt for Project A, since this is the one with the shortest pay back period. This decision would, however, take no account at all of the *profitability* of the projects. Nothing in the method used enables a comparison to be made between the relative desirability of the £10,000 cash flows from Project A over its four-year life and the cash flows of £16,100 from Project B over its ten-year life.

If one does consider the relative profitability of the two projects it can be seen that Project A in fact has a zero rate of return. It has done nothing more than replace the cash originally invested, i.e. £10,000 has been paid out and £10,000 received back. Project B on the other hand has a cumulative cash flow greater than the amount invested, and so it must have a positive rate of return, but the method used does not tell us what that rate is.

Clearly we have not progressed at all in our search for a method of arriving at a truly comparable rate of return, and the importance of the timing of receipts has once again been highlighted. The pay back method may have some uses in screening projects. If, for a variety of reasons, management wants to limit investment to short pay back projects, then it can be used to weed out those that do not fulfil the laid down criteria. However, those that do get through this screening must then be subject to ranking in order of profitability, and testing to ensure that projects approved do meet minimum rate of return criteria.

Residual value

So far we have concentrated upon the year-by-year profits or cash flow, but cash flows or adjustments to profits can arise at the end of a project when the assets that remain are disposed of. In most cases this will be an inflow of cash arising from the sale of those assets. But it can, of course, also be a further outlay, e.g. to decommission a nuclear power station, or to restore gravel workings.

In many cases these cash flows will be rather minor in relation to those arising from the remainder of the project, as they relate to worn out plant. But if there is a substantial working capital or land and buildings investment in the project, these values can be very significant. In any case they form a part of the total cash flows that arise from the project and must be taken into account when assessing its profitability.

Summary

A high level of long-term profitability can only be achieved by the directors of the business developing a long-term strategy for that business which identifies those areas where new investment is required to meet that company's long-term objectives. Within this overall framework there should then be a specific project selection process which enables management to select those projects earning the higher rates of return.

If management is to carry out the selection process in a rational way, the appraisal system adopted must provide for the proper evaluation of the amount of additional capital that must be locked up in a project. It must then provide for an assessment of the year-by-year increase in cash flows that will result from that investment over its life, including any residual values. All of these values must then be related in a way that will enable the decision-takers to rank the projects in order of profitability and ensure, as far as possible, that investments are not made in projects earning less than the cost of capital.

Any method of appraisal of capital investments has a vital role to play in maintaining or increasing the profitability of the business, both because of the long-term nature of such projects and the size of the funds that are often involved. The profitability of investments is just as important as the volume of investment, and within the individual firm the level of profitability achieved will be a major determinant of the volume of funds that can be made available in the future.

18

The more traditional methods of selection—the accounting rate of return and the pay back period—have certain flaws which can lead to them giving the wrong indication of profitability. On their own they do not fully take into account all the factors involved in an investment decision, and in some cases can be completely misleading, unless subject to further analysis. The one vital factor that has not been taken into account by either of the two methods is the timing and duration of the profits or cash flows. It is this timing factor to which we must now turn our attention, since it is crucial to an understanding of the basis of discounted cash flow.

2. *Present value*

The timing of cash flows is the key to any satisfactory measurement of the rate of return on an investment. In this chapter it is proposed to examine the implications of this timing concept and of the time value of money.

Time value of money

Remember that when talking of the time value of money, one is not dealing in any way with inflation and its consequences. We are simply considering the fact that if one is offered £10,000 with the opportunity of having it now or in three years time, inevitably one will opt to have it now, since money in hand now is more valuable than money receivable some time in the future, because that money has an earning power in the meantime. The more distant in time that receipt is, the less valuable will it be.

The investment projects undertaken by a business usually require the investment of a sum of money at the beginning of the project, hopefully followed by a stream of receipts of money over a series of years. If the time value of money is to be fully taken into account in the appraisal process, then the cash flow in each of those future periods of time must be valued on the same time basis as the original investment, i.e. to be shown at their respective values at the present time. What that present value should be will depend on the discount rate used and the time interval before they are received.

The pattern of cash flows

The pattern of cash flows associated with any project can be represented in the form of a cash flow diagram, such as that shown in Figure 2.1. If the cash flows are to be valued on a common time basis then one of the years must be selected as the base year. Since the decisions are being made now, i.e. the present time, it is usual to designate the year in which the investment is made as the base year for the project and treat it as neutral as far as timing is concerned. The other years are then numbered off from this base year.

The pattern of cash flows shown in Figure 2.1 represents a fairly simple project. Other investment projects will be of a much more complex nature. In the case of large construction projects there may be several years of construction, and therefore cash outflows, before it is commissioned and begins to generate positive cash flows. Furthermore, the long-term plans for that project may require capacity extensions to be made at specific future periods and these may turn the cash flows for those future years into negative flows rather than positive ones.

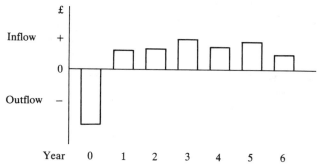

Figure 2.1 Cash flow diagram—simple project

This type of more complex project is represented in Figure 2.2. It illustrates a project where there is a three-year construction period covering years −2, −1, and 0. The project starts to earn revenues in year 1 and that continues in subsequent years, with the exception of years 5 and 8 when the installation of additional capacity results in net cash outflows, i.e. the new outlays exceed the returns from the existing plant.

Whether the investment project is simple or complex, the objective of DCF is the same—to evaluate the cash flows arising in each of the years to a common time basis, the year represented in Figures 2.1 and 2.2 by year 0. Cash flows arising in years subsequent to year 0 will need to be brought back to their value at that base year by means of discount factors that will reduce the value of the *future* receipts to their *present values* at the base year. In Figure 2.2 the investment period extends for more than one year and an interest or earnings factor must be *added* to the cost of the investment in years prior to year 0 to bring it to its value at the base year. Alternatively the first year of the investment period could be treated as year 0 and all other years numbered from there.

This process of relating the cash flows of all of the years to be base year value is illustrated in Figure 2.3. Each year's cash flow is brought back to its

Figure 2.2 Cash flow diagram—complex project

21

value at the base year, i.e. to its present value. This is the 'discounting' part of discounted cash flow. The present value is of course smaller than the future value because of its earning power in the intervening years. If there are expenditures prior to year 0, their value is increased to take account of the earning power that has been foregone.

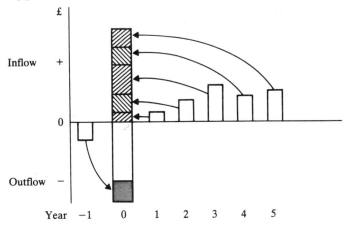

Figure 2.3 Process of relating cash flows to base year values

The assessment of the profitability of a project will then depend on the relationship between (1) the total of the positive cash flows that arise valued at their base year or present value, (2) the total of the negative cash flows also valued at their base year or present values, and (3) the percentage rate that has been used to discount the cash flows to their present values. These three elements are related in such a way that management can either (a) ascertain the rate of return that will be earned on the project, or (b) test whether that project meets minimum rate of return criteria. In the latter case a method must then be devised to rank in order of profitability.

Compound interest

Money can be put to use in many ways. It can be deposited with a building society, bank or other financial institution. It can be loaned to individuals or invested in companies so that they can use the money as part of the capital that they employ in their business. In all such cases the person lending or investing the money expects some return for its use, the usual form of return being the payment of interest, or, in the case of shareholdings in companies, a dividend. The owner of the funds may, on the other hand, decide to use those funds in his or her own business where it would be expected to produce a return in the form of an increase in the profits of that business.

Whenever money is put to a specific use, as distinct from being hidden under the mattress or held in a non-interest current account, it is done for a specific reason. The owner of that money believes that that use will increase the value of the money over time through earning interest or dividends, or increase its capital value, as in the case of investments in stocks and shares.

Suppose interest is compounded at yearly intervals, and one deposits £100 in a building society where it can earn, say, 7 per cent (ignoring tax), then at the end of one year the original £100 will have grown to £107. If nothing is withdrawn from the account, then at the end of the second year the amount on deposit will have grown to £114.49, i.e. [107 + (7 × 107/100)]. This process of accumulation will continue until such time as the money is withdrawn. If one needs to know to what value it will have grown over any particular period of time one can use the following formula:

Let i = interest rate per period
n = number of periods

Then

$$\text{Future value} = \text{Present value} \times (1 + i)^n$$

Compound interest can be used to solve a number of business problems. Suppose that money is available for investment in stocks of raw whisky which, after being held for maturing for five years, would be sold for blending. Management will expect that the sale of the whisky at the end of the fifth year will realize more money than was originally invested, since, over that period of time, the capital locked up could have earned a return if invested elsewhere. If money could earn 8 per cent from other forms of investment, then it might not be wise to invest money in uses where it earns less than that rate. It follows that if management is considering investing £1,000 in whisky stocks, then the anticipated realizable value of the whisky after the five-year period would need to be in excess of £1,470, which is the amount to which £1,000 would grow over five years if earning 8 per cent compounded annually.

Discounting

Discounting is calculated on the same basis as compound interest. Compound interest is used to take a sum of money invested now and calculate its value at a given time in the future. Discounting is used to take a sum of money receivable in the future and calculate what it is worth now, i.e. its *present value*.

If a business can earn 10 per cent on the funds that it uses, then, over a number of years, a sum invested of £100 would increase in value as follows:

23

Year 0	Year 1	Year 2	Year 3	Year 4	Year^n
£100	£110	£121	£133.1	£146.41	$£100(1 + 0.1)^n$

In such a case, a person or a business that could earn 10 per cent on their money would be indifferent as to whether they had £100 now, or received £110 in one year's time, or £121 in two year's time, and so on, because at an interest rate of 10 per cent these receipts would be of equal value when adjusted for the timing of the receipt. It must be emphasized again that one is only taking into account the *time value* of money and not any other factors such as inflation or uncertainty. These latter aspects will be dealt with at a later stage. All we are doing at this point is to examine preferences between the receipt of money at different times, on the basis of the earning power of that money.

The case where £100 will have grown to £110 at the end of one year is shown in Table 2.1 at (a), £100 invested on 1 January 1989 having grown to £110 by the end of the year. But just as interest or earning power can be used to calculate future values, one can use the same series of numbers to calculate *present values* through the process of discounting.

Table 2.1 Relationship between present and future values

	1 Jan. 1989 £		31 Dec. 1989 £
(a)	100	⟶	110
(b)	100	⟵	110
(c)	100/110	⟵	1
(d)	0.909	⟵	1

To say that £100 invested now will have become £110 in one year's time at 10 per cent is the same as saying that £110 receivable in one year's time has a present value of £100. Instead of looking forward from the present time to a future time, as shown at (a) in Table 2.1, we are merely looking backwards from a future time to the present, as shown at (b). To help with the process of calculation one can take the matter a further step forward. If £110, receivable in one year's time, has a present value of £100, then £1 receivable in one year's time is worth £100/110, or £0.909 now, since if £0.909 is invested now and earns 10 per cent, it will have grown to £1 by the end of one year.

This relationship between present and figure values can now be explored further. Table 2.1 set out the basic relationship between the two for a one-year period. Now consider a range of time periods. Continuing with the 10 per cent rate, we can use the same process over a series of years and arrive at a common basis for all calculations—the present value of £1 receivable at the end of x number of years, as shown in Table 2.2.

To calculate the present value of a future sum the following formula can be used:

$$\text{Present value} = \frac{\text{Future sum}}{(1+i)^n}$$

where i = interest rate per period
  n = number of periods.

Table 2.2 Present value of £1 receivable at varying times in the future

Year	Present value of £1 at 10% after the number of years		Year 0	Year 1	Year 2	Year 3	Year 4
			£100	£110	£121	£133.1	£146.41
0	£1	100/100	← £1				
1	£0.909	100/110	←	£1			
2	£0.826	100/121	←		£1		
3	£0.751	100/133.1	←			£1	
4	£0.683	100/146.41	←				£1

USE OF DISCOUNT TABLES

The rather tedious method of discounting future values using the formula above can be avoided by using tables of present value factors, such as that shown in Appendix A. This shows the present value of £1 receivable after different periods of time and for a range of discount rates. To use this table, first look along the top to find the rate of discount required. Then follow the column under that discount rate down to the number of years that will elapse before the money is to be received. The factor at that point is the factor by which the future sum must be multiplied to find its present value.

Take an example where a sum of £250 will be received after a period of eight years, and the rate of return is 6 per cent. First, locate the 6 per cent column, then follow that column down to the line for year eight. The factor at that point is 0.627. Therefore the present value of £250 receivable in eight years time is £250 × 0.627, or £156.75.

When the same sum of money is receivable in *each* of a series of years, then instead of discounting each year's receipt individually, the table in Appendix B can be used. This table shows the present value of £1 receivable *each year*, again for a range of years and discount rates. To find the present value of £54 receivable in each of the next ten years, using a discount rate of 8 per cent, first find the column for 8 per cent, then follow that column down to the line for the tenth year. This shows a factor of 6.710. To find the present value of £54 receivable annually simply multiply that sum by the factor, i.e. £54 × 6.710 = £362.34. The present value factors in the table in Appendix B are simply the cumulative of the values for each rate shown in Appendix A.

DCF or internal rate of return

One method of using DCF is to calculate the actual rate of return earned on the investment in a project during its life. It involves comparing the cash flows that will be generated by that project with the capital investment that it will require. The pattern of cash flows, both positive and negative, will be similar to that shown in Figures 2.1 and 2.2, i.e. there will normally be an outflow of cash at the beginning of the project as fixed assets or working capital are acquired, followed by a series of positive cash flows arising from the operations of the project.

The aim of the rate of return method is to find a percentage rate of discount that will produce a zero or near zero net present value for *all* the cash flows, i.e. the present value of the positive series of cash flows equals the investment. This is a trial and error method. Remember that the higher the discount rate used, the lower will be the present value of any sum receivable in the future. If one tries a discount rate and the present value of those future cash flows exceeds the investment then a higher discount rate must be used. If it is lower then a lower discount rate must be used. This process is continued until the discount rate that fits the project is found.

METHOD OF CALCULATING THE RATE OF RETURN

As an example of this process take a case where the investment of £200 now will result in cash flows of £115 arising in each of the next two years, i.e. there is a cash outflow of £200 in year 0, and an inflow of £115 in each of years 1 and 2. A discount rate must be found which will reduce the total present value of the cash flows in years 1 and 2 to as near to £200 as is reasonable.

One way of setting out the solution to the problem is shown in Table 2.3. Other methods of presentation will be used later in the book.

The first two columns of Table 2.3 show the identifying years and the cash flow for each year. The third column gives the discount factors for the 10 per cent discount rate for the relevant years (as shown in Appendix A). This is the rate which has been found by trial and error to fit the problem. Each year's cash flow is multiplied by the relevant factor to show the present value of that cash flow in the last column. This shows that the present value of the two years' cash flows is £199.5. As this is almost the

Table 2.3 Calculating the rate of return

Year	Cash flow £	Present value factors for 10%	Present value £
1	115	0.909	104.5
2	115	0.826	95.0
			199.5
Original sum invested			200.00

same as the investment it can be said that the rate of return on the project is 10 per cent.

MEANING OF THE RATE OF RETURN

What is meant when one says that the rate of return on a project is 10 per cent, or any other rate? A simple way of defining it is to say: 'If the cost of that pool of funds referred to in Figure 1.1 (or the cost of capital as we will be calling it later) is 10 per cent, then this project would just cover that cost.' A fuller definition is: 'The cash flows would repay the original investment and provide the stated rate of return on the amount of capital that remains invested in each year of the life of a project.' An understanding of this definition is essential if one is to understand the use of DCF in selecting projects.

That understanding can perhaps best be achieved by using the same values in a more familiar setting—that of borrowing money from a building society. If one wished to borrow £200 and repay that loan over two years, and the building society charges 10 per cent interest, then one would have to pay to the building society £115 in each of the two years. This is directly comparable with the DCF method since building societies calculate interest on the amount owed at the beginning of each year, and discounting uses the end of the year as its base.

The analysis of the cash flows for the loan is shown in Table 2.4. The two years' loan repayments provide for the repayment of the £200 borrowed *and* the provision of 10 per cent interest on the amount of the loan outstanding at the beginning of each of the years.

This analysis shows that the two years' cash flows (in this case the two loan repayments) have been sufficient to provide for the repayment of the £200 borrowed and the provision of 10 per cent interest on the loan outstanding at the beginning of each of the years (there is a small amount outstanding as the rate is not precisely 10 per cent).

It may help if one considers that the rate of return is what that project could afford to pay for the money that is being used to finance it. If you like

Table 2.4 Analysis of cash flows

		£	£
Amount borrowed			200.0
Year 1	Amount repaid	115.0	
	Of which £20 is the 10% interest on the amount owing at the beginning of the year	20.0	
	Leaving to be paid off the amount owed	95.0	
			95.0
	Amount owed carried forward to Year 2		105.0
Year 2	Amount repaid	115.0	
	Of which £10.5 is the 10% interest on the amount owing at the beginning of the year	10.5	
	Leaving to be paid off the amount owed	104.5	
			104.5
	Amount owed at the end of the year		0.5

we are looking at a project which is 'borrowing' £200 from the pool of funds financing the business, and what we are calculating in the rate of return is what that project could afford to pay for using those funds. This is why this DCF method is often called the *internal rate of return* (IRR), since it is entirely dependent on the cash flows of that particular project. Whenever one has calculated the DCF or internal rate of return for a project then this rate can be used for a similar calculation to that shown in Table 2.4, and at the end of the life of the project the value left should not be significant.

Example 2.1

The board of directors of Wendover plc is considering the possibility of purchasing a new lathe for £2,000. It has been estimated that this machine would increase operating cash flows by the following amounts:

Year	Cash flow £
1	500
2	500
3	600
4	600
5	440
Total	2,640

Before reaching a decision the directors have asked that the rate of return that would be earned on the project be calculated.

PRE-ESTIMATE OF THE RATE OF RETURN

While the DCF rate of return method requires a process of trial and error to arrive at a solution, that process can be shortened by making an estimate of what the rate may be. This estimate is based on the accounting rate of return method and suffers the same disadvantages. First, take the total positive cash flows and deduct from them the amount of the investment (this identifies the total profit from the project). Next divide this sum by the number of years' life of the project (which calculates the average annual profit). Then express this sum as a percentage of *half* the original investment (this gives the accounting rate of return based on average investment).

Using the data for Example 2.1, the estimate would be as follows:

1. Excess of cash flows over original investment: £2,640 − £2,000 = £640.
2. Divide (1) by the number of years' life: £640/5 = £128.
3. Calculate (2) as a percentage of *half* the original investment: 128 × 100/1,000 = 12.8%.

Remember that, as it is not based on compound interest, it will overstate the rate, and since it does not take timing into account, if the cash flows are skewed to the early years or the later years this will affect the rate of return. However, it may be of some help when deciding where to start on the discount rates.

Taking 12 per cent as the first approximation, this would give the result shown in Table 2.5. The discount factors for 12 per cent are extracted from Appendix A for the years 1 to 5. The cash flows for each of the years is multiplied by that year's present value factor to give its present value as shown in the last column. When these are totalled they give a present value for that series of cash flows of £1,903. Since this value is less than the

Table 2.5 Example 2.1: calculation of present values using 12% rate

Year	Cash flow £	Present value factors for 12%	Present values £
1	500	0.893	446
2	500	0.797	399
3	600	0.712	427
4	600	0.636	382
5	440	0.567	249
		Total	1,903

amount invested, this means that the 12 per cent rate is *too high*, and a lower discount rate should be tried.

If the 8 per cent rate is used for the next try, the calculations would be those shown in Table 2.6. In this case it is found that the sum of the present values is greater than the investment. This means that the 8 per cent rate is *not high enough* and therefore a higher rate should be used. It does mean, of course, that the actual rate of return must lie somewhere between 8 per cent and 12 per cent.

Table 2.6 Example 2.1: calculation of present values using 8% rate

Year	Cash flow £	Present value factors for 8%	Present value £
1	500	0.926	463
2	500	0.857	428
3	600	0.794	476
4	600	0.735	441
5	440	0.681	300
		Total	2,108

Where the actual rate of return has been bracketed as closely as by the two rates used so far, one could use a simple arithmetical interpolation to find the actual rate. In the example used so far the rate could be calculated as follows:

$$8\% + (4 \times 108/205) = 10.1\%$$

where 4 is the interval between the two rates used, 108 is the difference between the present value at the 8 per cent rate and the investment, and 205 is the difference between the two present values. What one is trying to do is to position the present value of the investment (which is of course its actual value) on the interval between the present values of the future cash flows using the two discount rates. The result is shown to one decimal place. Whether it should be shown to even one decimal place is debatable, as the cash flows used are, of course, only best estimates and have limited accuracy. The result should certainly not be taken to more than one decimal place.

If we now apply the 10 per cent rate to the problem it would appear as shown in Table 2.7. This shows that when discounting at the 10 per cent rate the present value of the future cash flows almost equals the investment—or the overall net present value is nearly zero.

Referring back to the definition of the rate of return, the above calculation means that the investment of £2,000 on a new lathe would generate additional cash flows sufficient to provide a 10 per cent return on the money locked

Table 2.7 Example 2.1: calculation of present values using 10% rate

Year	Cash flow £	Present value factors for 10%	Present value £
1	500	0.909	454
2	500	0.826	413
3	600	0.751	451
4	600	0.683	410
5	440	0.621	273
		Total	2,001

up in the project each year, and to repay the original investment of £2,000. A division of the cash flows between interest and principal along the lines used in Table 2.4 is given in Table 2.8. The small balance remains because the rate is not exactly 10 per cent.

Table 2.8 Example 2.1: division of cash flows between interest and principal

Year	Amount invested at beginning of year £	Cash flow £	10% interest on amount invested at beginning of year £	Balance of cash to reduce amount invested £	Amount invested at end of year £
1	2,000	500	200	300	1,700
2	1,700	500	170	330	1,370
3	1,370	600	137	463	907
4	907	600	91	509	398
5	398	440	40	400	(2)

USE OF THE RATE OF RETURN METHOD

Where the actual rate of return is calculated for each project management is able to look at the relative merits of a series of investment projects being considered. The DCF rate of return or IRR will enable them to apply the following criteria to the projects:

1. Which are the most profitable?
2. Do the projects meet the minimum rate of return?

In any given situation management then has the means of making a rational selection from the various alternatives available and allocate the funds of the business in the optimum way.

Present value method

The thinking behind the use of the present value method of using DCF is that decisions made about how funds should be deployed within the business should be made with the objective of maximizing the total net present value (NPV) of the business. This means that projects should be selected on the basis of the NPV that they generate—those with a higher NPV being selected rather than those with a lower NPV. The difficulty with this concept is that it does not take into account the capital that has to be deployed to earn that NPV, and unless some index of profitability is constructed that does take into account the amount of the investment, the results can differ from those given by the rate of return method.

Instead of finding the rate of return by trial and error, the present value method adopts the criterion rate for discounting the cash flows. This means that the net present value of the cash flows, i.e. the present value of the future flows less the investment, will be either positive or negative. If they are negative it means that the project does not meet the criterion rate; if they are positive it means that the rate of return is greater than the criterion rate and the project is acceptable, but it does not give any profitability ranking. To ensure that NPV on its own does not mislead the decision-maker, one should then calculate a *profitability index* which will provide a ranking in terms of profitability comparable to the rate of return method.

CRITERION RATE OF RETURN

The criterion rate of return used in the present value method should ideally be established by management as part of its long-term planning. As a very minimum it should be the cost of the pool of funds or cost of capital to the business. This concept of cost of capital will be discussed further in Chapter 12. It is, however, essentially the ongoing average cost of raising the mix of funds that is used to finance the business, such cost being made up of the interest cost of borrowed money, the dividends paid on preference and any other fixed dividend share capital, and the return on equity shareholders' funds that the business would have to offer if it wished to raise new equity in the market. Normally it will be the *average* cost of capital that will be used, although there may sometimes be special circumstances where the *marginal* cost may be appropriate.

The cost of capital should, however, only be a very minimum rate and any project earning a rate lower than that should not be accepted unless there are special considerations. The criterion rate should be higher than the cost of capital for two reasons. First, all projects contain uncertainty since they are all dealing with the future which is never certain, but some will entail greater risks than others so a higher criterion rate may be appropriate for those projects with higher risks. Secondly, some of the resources of a firm may

PRESENT VALUE

have to be invested in projects for which there is no measurable return, such as safety measures, recreational facilities and so on. Investment in projects earning a rate of return must provide something over the cost of capital to cover such uses.

Covering the cost of capital is, however, a passive method of setting the criterion rate. If management is doing its job properly, it should establish the rate as part of its positive planning of the business, looking at the level of profitability required to meet those plans and satisfy market needs should it need to raise capital. On a less positive note it may look at existing levels of profitability and if these are adequate extrapolate from these as necessary.

USING THE PRESENT VALUE METHOD
Whatever the basis may be by which management has set the criterion rate, the first step in evaluating a project by the present value method is to discount the cash flows arising in each year by the present value factors for that rate.

Example 2.2
The chairman of Oakley's plc has been presented with a proposal to build an extension to the factory and equip it with new woodworking plant at a cost of £50,000. The building would be a temporary one and would be demolished at the end of eight years.

After considering the proposal, the chairman called in his accountant and said to him, 'Before approving this investment I want to know what rate of return is being earned on the capital employed at the present time, and I need to be satisfied that this investment should earn a rate of return at least 1 per cent higher than that rate.' After analysing the company's accounts, the accountant established that the company was currently earning 10 per cent after tax on its capital employed. The criterion rate for the project would therefore be 11 per cent.

The cash flows forecast for the project, are as follows:

	£		£
Year 1	9,000	Year 5	11,000
Year 2	10,000	Year 6	11,000
Year 3	10,000	Year 7	10,000
Year 4	10,000	Year 8	10,000

The evaluation of the project is shown in Table 2.9. Alongside each year are listed the cash flows and the present value factors for 11 per cent appropriate for that year. As with the rate of return method the cash flows for each year are now multiplied by the present value factor for that year to arrive at each year's cash flow's present value. The sum of those present values amounts to £51,697. This sum is greater than the negative cash flow, i.e. the investment of £50,000, and therefore the project earns a rate of return greater than the

Table 2.9 Example 2.2: present value of cash flows using the criterion rate of return

Year	Cash flow £	Present value factors for 11%	Present value £
1	9,000	0.901	8,109
2	10,000	0.812	8,120
3	10,000	0.731	7,310
4	10,000	0.659	6,590
5	11,000	0.593	6,523
6	11,000	0.535	5,885
7	10,000	0.482	4,820
8	10,000	0.434	4,340
Total	81,000		51,697

criterion rate of 11 per cent and is an acceptable project. If the sum of the positive present values, using the criterion rate, had been less than the amount of the investment then the project would be rejected as not meeting the criterion rate.

PROFITABILITY INDEX

The present value method has so far only provided one of the answers required, namely does the project earn more than the criterion rate of return. What it has not provided is the means to rank projects in order of profitability so that a choice may be made between projects. As stated earlier, the NPV on its own may not give the right answer. The above project has a NPV of £1,697 (51,697 – 50,000) but that gives no indication of relative profitability. To do this we need to relate the NPV to the amount that has had to be invested to earn that NPV. This we can do by calculating the *profitability index.*

This index is based upon a comparison of the total present value of the positive cash flows with the negative outflow represented by the investment, as shown by the following formula:

$$\frac{\text{Present value of cash inflows}}{\text{Amount of investment}} = \text{Profitability index}$$

Using the figures from Table 2.9, the profitability of the project outlined in Example 2.2 would be:

$$\frac{£51,697}{£50,000} = 1.03 \text{ profitability index}$$

If the profitability index is less than 1 the project does not meet the criterion rate; if it is exactly 1 then the rate of return on the project exactly matches the criterion rate; if it is greater than 1 then the index gives an indication of relative profitability and should provide the same ranking as one would get from the DCF rate of return method.

Discounted pay back

If management wants to use the pay back method described in Chapter 1, a better way would be to base it upon the cash flows discounted by the criterion rate. For example, looking at the figures used in Table 2.9, it can be seen that the cumulative discounted cash flows would equal the investment about two-thirds of the way through the eighth year. However, this method still leaves out of the computation all cash flows arising after the pay back period.

Summary

In this chapter we have discussed the way in which the time value of money can be taken into account by valuing all the years' cash flows on a common time basis. That common time basis is the present, i.e. now. The present value of all future cash flows are arrived at by a process of discounting, and the discount tables have a direct relationship with compound interest tables. Money has an earning power over time, and it is this factor that is used in the DCF technique to evaluate an investment project.

This technique can be used in one of two ways:

1. To arrive at the actual rate of return for the project.
2. To arrive at the present value of the cash flows using a criterion rate of return, and then rank projects by means of a profitability index.

Both of these methods are designed to enable management to evaluate a series of projects on the basis of selecting the most profitable and setting a minimum rate of return below which projects will not be selected.

So far the examples that have been used have been based upon given cash flows, and once these are known the appraisal process is purely mechanical, following one of the two methods outlined. In real life the most difficult problem with investment projects is determining what the cash flows are. In part, of course, this is derived from the normal planning/budgeting process. There are, however, some special factors involved and these will be dealt with in the next section of the book.

Section 2

What are cash flows?

3. *The implications of taxati*

At first sight the introduction of such a specialized topic as taxation into a book that deals with capital investment appraisal techniques may seem to be unnecessary. However, in almost every country today businessmen are faced with a comprehensive system of taxation that impinges on the decisions that are taken relating to their businesses. Decisions that in other respects might be the right ones can turn out to be unsound when the implications of taxation are taken into account, and vice-versa. It is questionable whether a business should be obliged to tailor its decisions in the light of tax considerations rather than make those decisions purely on commercial criteria. However, the business exists in the real world where tax systems may alter and rates of tax change, both of which may have important effects on the amount and timing of cash flows which must be taken into account.

As far as the appraisal of investment projects is concerned it must be remembered that it is the *after-tax* cash flows that will be used as the basis for the decision-making. There will, therefore, be a number of tax implications to be considered. It is almost universally true that a substantial part of the earnings of a project will require increased payment of taxes to the revenue authorities. That payment of tax may not coincide with the year in which the extra profits are earned. For example, in the United Kingdom the corporation tax on one year's profits are paid in the following year. Other countries may have a system of current collection of tax, as in the USA. Whatever the system the business operates under, it will have to take into account in its project appraisal any timing difference between the earning of profits and the payment of tax on those profits.

Apart from the taxation of profits, many countries provide a system of incentives to encourage investment in new tangible fixed assets, and for the writing off of the cost of those assets against profits. In the United Kingdom over the last twenty years there have been a number of systems using different rates, the present rates coming into existence as late as the 1986/87 tax year. When assets are sold adjustments will be made to the allowances given which will have implications for cash flow.

In addition to the factors already mentioned there is the possibility that gains on the sale of assets may be taxed, and in the EC and other countries valued added and similar taxes may affect cash flows. Many countries offer cash and tax incentives to attract new businesses into their territory, or designated areas within their territory, such as enterprise zones, all of which will have an important impact on the investment decision. Although management may need to call in taxation specialists for the more detailed aspects of any decision, a broad appreciation of the implications of taxation in relation to investment projects is necessary as part of the decision-making process.

In order to provide this general appreciation we will look at taxation under the following headings:

1. Taxation of income
2. The effect of incentives and reliefs relating to investment in fixed tangible assets
3. The taxation of capital gains
4. Other taxes

These topics will not be developed into a specialized discourse on taxation, rather our discussion will be confined to general terms and only touch on those aspects that may have to be taken into account when using DCF. Taxation today is a highly complex subject, and what is said here may not apply in special situations. In any case professional advice should be sought wherever there is any doubt about the tax position.

Taxation of profits

PARTNERSHIPS AND INDIVIDUALS
In the United Kingdom the taxation of trading profits for a partnership or sole trader is governed by the Income and Corporation Taxes Act 1988, as amended. The income of such individuals is subject to the payment of income tax and, where appropriate, any higher rate of tax.

Basis of assessment and payment of tax—continuing businesses
Where a partnership or individual has been trading for some years, the basis of assessment for the tax payable in any tax year is the taxable profits of the business for its accounting period *ended* in the *previous tax year*. Income tax is the only tax payable on such income and the amount paid may be reduced by personal reliefs.

Assume that Mr A owns a business that has been earning profits for several years. For his accounting year which ended on 31 December 1989 the profits earned, adjusted for tax purposes, amounted to £20,000. The business is Mr A's sole source of income. For the tax year 1990/91, the assessment will be based on the £20,000 profit for the accounting year to 31 December 1989. The actual amount of tax payable will be at the basic rate plus, if the income is high enough, any higher rate of tax, subject to the personal allowances and reliefs available. The tax will be paid in two instalments on 1 January 1991 and 1 July 1991.

It follows from this that non-incorporated businesses will experience a time delay between earning profits and paying the tax based on that level of profit. According to the date adopted for the businesses' accounting year end, that payment will fall due either in the year following the earning of the profit, or the year after that.

Basis of assessment and payment early—and closing years
For the tax year in which a business is started, the assessment of tax is based on the proportion of the taxable profits of the first period's trading which fell within that tax year.

Example 3.1

Mr A starts trading on 1 January 1988, and his first year's trading ends on 31 December 1988. The taxable profits for that period amount to £40,000. Since the business started trading in the tax year 1987/88 there will be an assessment to tax for that year. This will be based on $\frac{1}{4}$ (three months) of £40,000, or £10,000.

For the tax year following that in which the business was set up the assessment will be based on the taxable profits for the first twelve months' trading. Using the figures for Example 3.1 the assessment on Mr A for the tax year 1988/89 will be £40,000, being the taxable profits of the first year's trading.

In the subsequent tax year, the basis of assessment reverts to the normal continuing basis set out earlier. So for the tax year 1989/90 Mr A's assessment to tax will be based on the first year's trading, the accounting period of which ended in the previous tax year, and will be £40,000.

As can be seen the first year's profits will generally determine the tax liability for the first three tax years during which the business is trading; the main exception is where the accounting period exactly coincides with the tax year, when it will form the basis for only two years' assessments. When the first three years trading are complete the taxpayer has a further choice. He or she can, if it is to their advantage, elect to have the assessments for 1988/89 and 1989/90 amended to the actual profits earned in those tax years.

In the closing years of the business the final year's assessment is based on the taxable profits earned during that tax year; if the total sum already assessed for the penultimate and pre-penultimate years is lower than the actual profits of those years, the Inland Revenue have the option to revise those assessments to the actual profits earned during those tax years.

Rate
The current (1988/89) basic rate of tax is 25 per cent with a single higher rate of 40 per cent.

CORPORATIONS

For the purposes of corporation tax, the term 'corporation' includes not only limited companies and other incorporated bodies, but also a number of unincorporated bodies, such as clubs.

Basis of assessment

The basis of assessment to corporation tax is the accounting period of the company. If the company's accounting period runs from 1 January to 31 December 1990, the adjusted profits for that period will form the basis for the taxation period running from 1 January to 31 December 1990. The period 1 January to 31 March 1990 falls in the corporation tax year 1989 (the corporation tax year is dated by the year in which it starts). The period 1 April 1990 to 31 December 1990 falls in the corporation tax year 1990.

Where there is no change in the corporation tax rate between the two years an assessment will simply be raised on the adjusted profits for the accounting period and the tax due will be paid nine months after the end of the accounting period.

Where the corporation tax rate changes between the two tax years, then the company's profits are time apportioned between the two years and each part charged at the appropriate rate.

Assume that APC plc had taxable profits for its accounting year to 31 December 1990 of £600,000. Assume the corporation tax rate for 1989 was 40 per cent and for 1990 was 35 per cent. The tax payable on the profits of the company for that year would be calculated as follows:

	Taxable profits £	*Tax rate* %	*Tax payable* £
Corporation tax year 1989 ($\frac{1}{4}$ of £600,000)	150,000	40	60,000
Corporation tax year 1990 ($\frac{3}{4}$ of £600,000)	450,000	35	157,500
	600,000		217,500

Subject to any advance corporation tax related to dividends the tax owing would be paid on 1 October 1991 under present rules.

Rate

The current (1989) rate of corporation tax is 35 per cent. There is a special rate for small companies of 25 per cent. A small company in this context is one with taxable profits of less than £150,000. There is marginal relief for companies in the band £150,000 to £750,000 with the lower rate gradually being phased out until at the £750,000 level the normal rate is paid on all profits.

It follows from the above that where the UK type of system operates the tax on profits earned in one accounting period will not be paid until the following accounting period. Under other tax regimes that tax may be payable on a modified 'pay as you earn basis'.

Capital allowances (depreciation)

Allowances for expenditure on tangible fixed assets will be regulated by the fiscal laws of the country in which the business operates. In most countries, providing the methods and rates of depreciation used in the accounts comply with the tax regulations, then the charge is allowable. In addition to regulating the methods and rates of depreciation, the tax regime may provide incentives for new capital expenditure either through direct cash grants or by providing for some form of acceleration in the granting of depreciation relief.

In the UK, whether one is taxed to income or corporation tax, the depreciation charged in the accounts is disallowed for tax purposes. To arrive at the taxable profits the amount charged for depreciation must be added to the net profit as shown below for XYL plc:

Items extracted from XYL plc profit and loss account

	£000s
Gross profit	15,000
Depreciation	- 2,000
Other expenses	- 3,000
Net profit	10,000

Subject to any other adjustments the taxable profit of XYL plc will be:

	£000s
Net profit as per accounts	10,000
Add back depreciation	2,000
	12,000

Two points emerge from this treatment of depreciation. First, under the UK type of system, the basis used for the depreciation charge in the business's accounts will have no effect on the tax that will be paid. Second, when computing the cash flows for DCF, depreciation should not be deducted from the increased profits. Thus the increase in profits before depreciation, i.e. the operating cash flows (see Appendix C), equals the taxable profits before deducting the allowances that are given in place of depreciation. In the UK these are called *capital allowances*.

UNITED KINGDOM CAPITAL ALLOWANCES
Plant and machinery
The system currently in force provides for a single allowance to be given each year in respect of which an asset is owned. Where an asset is purchased

Table 3.1 The 'pool' account

	'Pool' £000s	Writing-down allowances £000s
Balance at 1 January 1989	9,000	
Sales proceeds of disposals for year to 31 December 1989	1,000	
	8,000	
Plus cost of acquisitions for year to 31 December 1989	4,000	
Pool balance 31 December 1989	12,000	
Annual writing-down allowances for the year to 31 December 1989, 25% of £12,000	3,000	3,000
Pool balance carried forward	9,000	

at any time during the year the full year's allowance can be claimed. The allowances given for plant and machinery (which includes fixtures and fittings, furnishings and vehicles) are called annual writing-down allowances, and the rate at the present time (1989) is 25 per cent on the reducing balance.

'Pooling'
All such assets, other than motor cars, are put into a 'pool' at its cost price, and the year-by-year capital allowances will be calculated on the 'pool' balance (motor cars will have their own 'pool' account). The 'pool' balance at any one time represents the total value of past expenditures on plant and machinery, less the capital allowances claimed, and also less the sale proceeds of any disposals of assets. (This is illustrated in Table 3.1.) This means that at the end of the day the capital allowances given for any item of expenditure will be limited to the difference between what it cost and what it was sold for.

If one now refers back to the example of XYL plc used earlier, the adjusted profits for tax purposes would be as follows:

	£000s
Net profit per accounts	10,000
Add back depreciation	2,000
	12,000
Less Capital allowances	3,000
Adjusted profits for tax purposes	9,000

Balancing charge

It will be noted from the above that when an asset is sold or scrapped, any proceeds from the disposal reduces the 'pool' balance. Should this produce a negative 'pool' balance, then that figure becomes an addition to the taxable profit for that year called a balancing charge. Should the sale proceeds of a particular asset exceed its cost, the excess over the cost is a capital gain.

Buildings

Businesses can claim a writing-down allowance in respect of expenditure on industrial buildings (i.e. factories, warehouses, etc., and some repair shops). Offices, shops, etc., get no relief for the expenditure. Up to 25 per cent of the capital cost can relate to non-qualifying uses without restricting the allowance.

The rate of writing-down allowance for industrial buildings is 4 per cent of the original cost. In enterprise zones 100 per cent of the cost can be claimed in the year of acquisition. In this case offices and shops are also included. There are other schemes for hotels, agricultural buildings, etc., to which reference should be made as appropriate.

CARRY FORWARD OF UNUSED CAPITAL ALLOWANCES

Where a business makes a loss or a level of profit insufficient to absorb the benefit of all the capital allowances, and they cannot be relieved in any other way, they can be carried forward and offset against future profits from the same trade. Individuals may be able to offset them against other income of the tax year.

EFFECT OF GRANTS AND CAPITAL ALLOWANCES ON CASH FLOW

Cash flow computations must take into account the following factors related to the acquisition and ownership of tangible fixed assets:

1. Are there any direct financial subsidies available which will reduce the actual cost of the assets? The net cash investment must be reduced by the amount of any such receipts.
2. Are there any methods of obtaining depreciation or capital allowances early in the life of the asset. If so, they can be used to increase the cash flows in the early years when they are more valuable.
3. The year by year depreciation or writing-down allowances will reduce the taxable profits of those years and therefore the cash outflow for tax payments.
4. When an asset is sold one will have to take into account not only the cash

from the sale, but also the cash flow implications of any consequential adjustment to capital allowances.

5. What is the timing of the above cash flow effects?

Capital gains tax (CGT)

Where a business sells a fixed asset for more than its cost a liability arises for CGT. Capital gains are now taxed in the UK as income of individuals at the relevant tax rate, and for companies as income at the relevant corporation tax rate. There are special provisions for assets used in a trade. These are known as *roll-over* provisions, the practical effect of which is that a continuing business can carry forward all or part of the liability for CGT indefinitely.

When the business sells an asset and realizes a capital gain, if an amount equal to the sale proceeds is invested in assets in the same trade within the previous year or the following three years, the gain can be deducted from the cost of those new assets. This of course increases the CGT liability when those assets are finally sold, but the roll-over process can be repeated over an indefinite series of such transactions.

Assets purchased prior to April 1982 can have their cost rebased on the March 1982 value. That cost can then be indexed by the Retail Price Index increase to the date of disposal. It follows from all of the above provisions that only in exceptional cases will there be an immediate liability for CGT, and therefore a cash flow for that payment.

Value added tax (VAT)

This tax operates in a similar way throughout the EC. As far as the acquisition of fixed assets is concerned, VAT will not affect the long-term cash flows of businesses that are not exempted from VAT. Although VAT will be added to the invoiced cost of the asset when purchased, that charge can be recovered by deduction from the VAT charged to the firm's own customers. The only exception to this is in the case of motor cars, where no deduction of input tax is allowed.

Businesses that are exempted from VAT bear the cost of that tax, and therefore the cost of fixed tangible assets that they purchase will include the cost of VAT.

Summary

When appraising any investment project the effects of taxation and any other governmental intervention must be taken into account. In spite of the

46

specialization even among tax experts, managers should have a broad appreciation of the possible tax consequences of their decisions. The more sophisticated analysis can be left to the professional who can assess the implications for any investment decision on the business as a whole. Management's broad appreciation should enable them to call for proper advice at the right stage of the appraisal, before any final decision is made, rather than leave taxation to be sorted out later.

A variety of tax systems and rates will be used in the examples in the remainder of this book.

4. *Determining the cash flows*

All investment decisions are about making choices. It may be a choice between doing nothing and carrying out a particular project; it may be a choice between different ways of carrying out the same project, or between different ways of financing it. In all cases the cash flows that are relevant are those which occur under one alternative, but do not occur under the other. A cash flow which is common to both choices is not relevant to the decision. So what one is trying to identify in each case is the *incremental cash flows* for that project.

What are cash flows?

Those who are accustomed to reading reports on companies in the financial press will be familiar with the term *cash flow*. As applied to the reports made by companies to their shareholders it covers the cash generated by the operations of the business for the year. This is of interest to investors and other users of company reports and is set out in the *sources and application of funds statement*. This statement starts with the profit of the business and adds back to that figure any expenses charged in arriving at that profit which do not involve cash outflows. The principal expense in that category is depreciation.

A shorthand definition of operating cash flow is therefore profit plus depreciation. The layman may find this definition confusing as *per se* there is no cash flow for depreciation. A fuller definition would be the cash flows from sales or similar activities, less those expenses involving cash outflows. A fuller explanation of the relationship between depreciation and cash flows is given in Appendix C.

As used in DCF, cash flows will be defined as the pre-tax profits of the project, plus the depreciation charge, and less any net extra tax payable attributable to that project. Readers will note that this definition coincides with the way profits are dealt with under the UK tax system, where profits are adjusted by adding back depreciation as shown on page 43 of Chapter 3, and are then reduced by capital allowances. DCF will, however, have to take into account any *timing* differences in the items that make up that after-tax cash flow. Whereas company accounts include the items in the relevant accounting period, when preparing cash flow measurements the income, depreciation, capital allowance and tax components must be shown separately and allocated to the years when the cash flow related to that item actually occurs.

This concept of cash flow is of vital importance to capital investment appraisal since the real cost to a business of any new investment project is the actual *net amount of cash* that flows out of the business as a result of that investment decision, and the return is made up of the net cash inflows to it during the life and at the end of the project.

DISTINCTION BETWEEN CASH FLOW AND ACCOUNTING ENTRIES

The cash outlay on a new project may, in a number of cases, be the same as the book cost shown in the accounts, and may also appear in the same accounting period. For example, where the investment is the simple purchase of an additional new machine, then the cash outlay and the book cost are the same and would appear in the same accounting period, unless there is some element of deferral in the purchase price.

In many cases, however, this will not be true. When a project involves the replacement of existing plant the issue is not so clear cut. The cash out-flow for the purchase of the new plant will be the same as the book value as before, but if there are any cash proceeds from the disposal of the replaced asset this will have to be taken into account. Note that it is the cash proceeds from the sale that are relevant, not the book value of the old plant. Also, as stated in the previous chapter, there may also be adjustment to the capital allowances on that disposal that will have cash flow consequences.

When considering the measurement of the cash flows during the life of a project, the annual operating cash flows will differ from those shown in the accounts. This is not because different basic figures are used, but because the cash flows used for DCF will be allocated to the period in which the cash movement actually takes place. So while, for example, the tax charge for the period will be shown as a charge in that year's accounts, in a tax system like that used in the UK, the payment of that tax will not take place until the following year. Overall, though, for any project, the book values will equal the cash flows, as will be shown later in this chapter; the difference between the two will only arise because of the timing differences.

INCREMENTAL PRINCIPLE

The remarks made so far in this chapter have highlighted the basic guideline to use when measuring cash flows—that it is the cash flow differences that we are concerned with, not absolute cash flows. When we are dealing with a particular investment project it is necessary to evaluate the *net* changes in the cash position of the business that would ensue if we go ahead with that project.

Consider the upgrading of a product to make it more competitive or to extend its profitable life, and which will continue to use the company's facilities. The cash flows used in the appraisal should not be the total investment in that product and the facilities required to produce it, nor the total operating cash flows during its life. They will be based upon the *extra* cash that will have to be invested to update the product and its production facilities, and the *additional* operating cash flows arising from the product over and above those that would have been earned if the updating does not take place. There may also be changes in the residual values and their timing that would result from the decision.

The extra cash flows invested in the product will consist of the outward payments for new research, plant and equipment, and any increase in working capital, less any amounts that may be released through the disposal of assets. The extra operating cash flows would be those that would be earned by the updated product less those that will be lost by dropping the old unimproved product. In all cases it is the cash flow difference with which we are concerned. Whatever the type of problem for which we are seeking a solution this incremental principle must always be kept in mind. One must also examine and measure *all* the cash flow consequences of the choices being considered.

TYPES OF CASH FLOW

The cash flows that must be quantified for the purposes of DCF are as follows:

1. *Net cash investment.* This is a measure of the *net* cost to cash resources of the new investment.
2. *Annual cash flows.* These represent the operating cash flows and tax consequences from the project which provide for the recoupment of the original investment and provide the return (if any) that is earned by the project.
3. *Net residual value.* This comprises the various cash flow consequences arising from the disposal of assets at the end of the life of the project, or decommissioning and reinstatement costs.

These three aspects of cash flow calculation will be looked at separately in this chapter. Each has different factors involved in its calculation and it is useful to divide the overall framework to the solution of a problem into these three distinctive aspects. At the end of the day, of course, they are all relevant to the overall cash flows arising from a project.

Net cash investment

The term *net cash investment* is used to denote the net outflow of cash that would result from the investment decision. It is therefore a measure of the amount of money that management would have to commit to a particular project, and against which the return will be measured. This concept of the 'cost' of an investment project is used rather than its book cost. For example, if an asset is to be replaced, it is the cash proceeds of that disposal that are offset against the cost of the new assets and not the book value of the asset sold.

ACQUISITION OF FIXED ASSETS

A major element of the net cash investment is likely to be the purchase of the fixed tangible assets that are required, such as plant and machinery, buildings, etc., together with any costs incurred on installation, modification, and commissioning. Where there is a running-in period the costs incurred during this period should also be included. The basic principle to be followed is that all expenditure incurred in getting the facilities into an operational state should be included.

The new project may also include the use of items of plant and equipment, etc., that the business already owns, and which, but for the decision to go ahead with the project, would be considered surplus to requirements and sold. The realizable cash value of these assets should be included in the net cash investment. Although there is no actual cash outlay for such assets, what is happening is that the business is foregoing the receipt of cash from the sale proceeds, and, as a result of the new project, will be worse off in cash terms if it goes ahead with the project.

Similar considerations apply where the new project will use some assets which would have otherwise been redeployed to other uses within the business. Because of this project going ahead those other uses may now have to be satisfied by the acquisition of other assets. Logically that cash outflow should also be considered as part of the cost of the investment.

PROMOTION COSTS OF NEW PRODUCTS

Launching a new product can involve the business in considerable outlays of cash for market research and other promotional activities. Such costs must be taken into account in the appraisal of a project.

WORKING CAPITAL

In addition to the fixed tangible assets used for the project, it is also probable that there will be a change in the level of working capital. Where the project is centred upon the production and sale of a new, additional product, this will almost certainly be the case. Investing £1 million in working capital is just as much an investment as buying a new machine for £1 million—both must earn the required rate of return.

Following the incremental principle, it is the *additional* amount that has to be invested in working capital items, such as stocks and debtors, that is relevant to the project under consideration. The substitution of one form of working capital for another is not sufficient to warrant the inclusion of an amount for this item as the two balance each other.

TREATMENT OF ASSETS REPLACED

The proposed new investment may also involve the disposal of some assets presently owned by the business. The cash proceeds from such a disposal must be offset against the cash outlays.

SUNK COSTS

Sunk costs, i.e. costs that have already been incurred and which cannot be recovered, must not be taken into account in the cash flows. The cash for these costs has already been paid out and irrespective of whether or not the business goes ahead with the new project those outlays will not be changed. For example, if the project concerns the launch of a new product, and by the time that project comes up for consideration the firm has already spent £2 million on development work for that product, that £2 million is not relevant to the decision as to whether or not to proceed further. It is an outlay that is common to both of the alternatives under consideration and is not therefore a cash difference between the two.

Example 4.1

The board of directors of Seetops plc is considering the position of the company when the lease of its present factory expires. In view of the imminence of the opening of the Channel Tunnel and the final integration of the EC in 1992, a proposal has been made that it should build a modern purpose-built factory in South East England to replace its existing premises. The cost of building and equipping the new factory is estimated to be £1.25 million. On completion of the move some of the existing plant and the balance of the lease would be sold and should realize £450,000. The new factory is expected to have an output 50 per cent greater than the old factory and will require an extra £250,000 investment in working capital to support that higher level of activity. Tax considerations are to be ignored at this stage.

For this project the net cash investment would be:

	£
Cost of new factory and plant	1,250,000
Less Sale of old plant, etc.	450,000
	800,000
Additional working capital	250,000
Net cash investment	1,050,000

The above treatment of replaced plant is appropriate if we are considering whether to replace the plant or not. Different considerations will apply if the decision to replace the plant has been made and the problem now being addressed is *how* the new plant should be acquired. Do we buy the new plant outright; do we lease the plant, or hire purchase, and so on. With this type of decision the net cash investment would simply be the cost of the new plant plus the extra working capital. No account would be taken of the sale value of the plant being replaced, since this cash flow will occur whichever method of acquiring the plant that we use. Once again it is being emphasized that it is only the cash flow *differences* that are relevant to the decision. (See Chapter 6, Alternative choice problems.)

TAX TREATMENT OF ASSETS SOLD

When one of the elements of the net cash investment is the sale of existing assets, then any tax consequences of that disposal should also be taken into account. As was seen in Chapter 3, when plant and equipment are sold, the capital allowances given are restricted to the difference between the original cost and the net proceeds from the disposal. If the sale proceeds produce a negative value on the 'pool' account this must be treated as a balancing charge and added to profits thus increasing tax payments. If it leaves a positive value on the 'pool' account then it will simply have reduced the future 25 per cent annual writing-down allowances.

From the point of view of the individual project if an asset with a written-down value for tax purposes of £50,000 is sold for £60,000, then £10,000 of the capital allowances already given will be clawed back, thus increasing future tax payments. If that asset was sold for £20,000, then it means that a further £30,000 of capital allowances will be given. The problem as far as DCF is concerned is that, except in the case where an immediate adjustment has to be made by way of a balancing charge, the effect on the 'pool' account will be to change the value of the ongoing stream of allowances indefinitely into the future. The only practical way to deal with this is to assume that the whole of the capital allowance adjustment takes place in the year of the disposal or the following year, unless the values are so significant that the full effect must be shown.

Example 4.2

Taking the same figures as those used in Example 4.1, the written-down value for tax purposes of the old machinery is £180,000 and the sale proceeds for this part of the disposal is £250,000.

The make-up of the net cash investment can now be shown as follows:

	£	£
Net cash investment		
Cost of new factory and plant		−1,250,000
Less Net proceeds of sale of old plant:		
Cash received	+450,000	
Adjustment to capital allowances	− (24,500)	
(£250,000 − 180,000 × 35% tax)		+ 425,500
		− 824,500
Additional working capital		− 250,000
Total		−1,074,500

REGIONAL GRANTS, ENTERPRISE ZONES, ETC.
Where government provides incentives for firms to locate in a particular
area, then any cash flow consequences of such incentives must be taken into
account. They may be in the form of direct cash grants that can be directly
identified, or they may result in the reduction of tax payments to local or
central government.

PROJECTS WITH LONG START-UP TIMES
Where the project is one which requires a number of years to construct the
buildings and plant before they become operational, the question arises as to
which of these years of cash outflows is to be treated as the base year for
timing purposes. One way would be to treat the year prior to becoming operational as the base year. The years prior to this would be numbered year −1,
year −2, and so on. In which case compound interest would have to be added
to the cash flows in those years to bring them to their base year value. The
trend today is to use the first of those years as the base year with all the years
of the project numbered from that base year. This means that there will be
one or more years after the base year with large cash outflows.

TIMING OF CASH OUTFLOWS FOR NET INVESTMENT
The cash flows for the net cash investment must be allocated to the years in
which those cash flows will actually take place. Where the project is a
straightforward purchase of a piece of plant which the firm is buying outright, then the year of purchase and the year of payment for that purchase are
likely to be the same. For more complex projects this might not be the case.
The situation where outright payment for the plant etc. is not made will be
considered later in this book in Chapter 6. There may, however, be other
factors such as:

1. Because of the length of the construction period the series of payments
   for the new plant are spread over a number of years, and the probability
   is that the purchaser will retain some of the contract monies for a period
   of time.
2. Where the values are significant, the tax consequences of the disposal of
   old plant may need to be taken over a number of years rather than
   straight away.

Example 4.3
Using the same data as that used in Examples 4.1 and 4.2, let us assume that
the construction period is two years, and that the client will be able to retain
10 per cent of the contract cost for one year after completion. £0.5 m of the
construction costs will be in the first year and the balance in the following
year. A criterion rate of 8 per cent is being used by the company.

Using this additional information the net cash investment could be restated as follows:

	£	£
Net cash investment		
Year 0		
Cost of new buildings and plant		
(£500,000 – 10%)		−450,000
Year 1		
Cost of new buildings and plant		
(£750,000 – 10%)	−675,000	
Sale proceeds of old plant[1]	+450,000	
	————	−225,000
Year 2		
Cost of new buildings and plant		
(retentions)	−125,000	
Additional working capital	−250,000	
Adjustment to tax allowances[2]	− 24,500	
	————	−399,500
Total		−1,074,500

Notes: 1. It is assumed that this is received in this year. 2. This adjustment should be at least one year later than the sale proceeds. If thought significant it could be spread over future years through the 'pool' account.

When dealing with the appraisal of this project these cash flows would now be discounted by the PV factors for 8 per cent for the relevant years.

Example 4.4

Porton plc are considering relocating a specialist automated production line. They have considered the offers made by a number of different countries' development agencies and have decided to move the line to a country which offers to give a grant of 40 per cent of the cost of the plant. However, because of the red tape involved it is not likely that the grant would be received until the year following the investment.

The cost of the new plant is expected to be £500,000. The existing equipment will be sold and should realize £15,000, and they have a written-down value for tax purposes of £40,000. The company uses a 10 per cent criterion rate, and the tax rate in the country involved is 40 per cent.

The net cash investment for this project would be calculated as follows:

55

	£	£
Net cash investment		
Year 0		
Cost of new plant		−500,000
Sale of old plant		+ 15,000
		−485,000
Year 1		
Grant receivable	+200,000	
Adjustment to tax allowances		
(£40,000 − 15,000) × 35%[1]	+ 8,750	
		+208,750
		−276,250

Note: 1. In this case the adjustment is a positive cash flow since the written-down value is greater than the sale value, thus providing extra tax allowances. It is assumed that the existing plant is in the UK and therefore the UK rate of tax would be relevant.

Annual cash flows

Under this heading we are dealing with changes in the cash position of the business which result from the operations of the new project. These cash flows are made up of three basic components:

1. the increased operating cash flows resulting from higher profits before depreciation, or from cost savings;
2. the extra tax payments that result from the higher level of profits before depreciation;
3. the impact that the system of capital allowances or giving depreciation allowances will have on the taxable profit.

INCREASE IN OPERATING CASH FLOWS

The increase in operating cash flows—which we have defined as basically profit before charging depreciation—will normally occur in the year in which the extra profits accrue. Only in exceptional cases will there be timing differences. Extra cash will be received from the extra sales made, less of course any expenses involving cash outflows, or cash outflows will be reduced by cost savings.

In practice, of course, credit is given for sales, or taken for purchases, stocks are held for production, and so on. These are, however, essentially *working capital* changes and will be dealt with as such.

56

TAXATION ON THE INCREASE IN OPERATING CASH FLOWS

If the operating cash flows will be increased by the project, then the business will have to pay extra taxes. Our next problem then is to consider the amount and timing of such extra taxes. In the UK, corporation tax is payable in the year after the extra profits are earned (for partnerships and individuals this period may be two years after the profits are earned), and these timing differences must be taken into account when measuring the cash flows. If the business operates under a tax regime where there is an element of 'pay as you earn' in the taxation of businesses then these timing differences may be smaller or not exist at all.

The profits that are taxed are after deducting depreciation, or, in the UK, capital allowances in lieu of depreciation. Where an asset is 'brought into use' during the year, even though that period of use may be only a day, then the whole of the first year's capital allowances can be claimed for that year. This means that it may be the case that the first year's capital allowances can be claimed in the year in which the investment is made, the year that we have been denominating year 0. It will probably be necessary therefore to deal with the taxation cash flows relating to the extra operating cash flows (profit before depreciation) separately from those relating to the capital allowances.

Example 4.5

AB plc proposes to invest £200,000 in new machinery and will be claiming the normal UK capital allowances. It is expected that the new machines will be replaced at the end of six years. The extra operating cash flows that are expected to be generated from the project are as follows:

Year	£
1	40,000
2	50,000
3	60,000
4	60,000
5	50,000
6	40,000

The make-up of the annual cash flows for the project together with the cash investment required are given in Table 4.1.

Residual value

At the end of the life of the project any assets that remain will be disposed of, either by sale, or being scrapped, or put to other uses within the business. In the same way as the project was charged with the related cash outflows at

Table 4.1 Example 4.5: cash flow table

Year	0 £000s	1 £000s	2 £000s	3 £000s	4 £000s	5 £000s	6 £000s	7 £000s
(a) Investment	-200.00							
(b) Operating cash flows		40.00	50.00	60.00	60.00	50.00	40.00	
(c) Extra tax @ 35% payable on (b)		—	-14.00	-17.50	-21.00	-21.00	-17.50	-14.00
'Pool' a/c								
(d) Added to pool	*200.00*							
(e) Capital allowances	*-50.00*	*-37.50*	*-28.13*	*-21.09*	*-15.82*	*-11.87*	*-8.90*	
(f) Pool balance	*150.00*	*112.50*	*84.38*	*63.28*	*47.46*	*35.60*	*26.70*	
(g) Tax saved by capital allowances ((f)×35%)		17.50	13.13	9.84	7.38	5.54	4.15	3.11
(h) Cash flow for year (a)+(b)+(c)+(g)	-200.00	57.50	49.13	52.34	46.38	34.54	26.65	-10.89

Notes:
1. Line (c) is stepped back one year to allow for the year's delay in paying tax. This means that year 7 has been added to accommodate this delay.
2. Line (e) is based on the assumption that the first year's capital allowances can be claimed in year 0. This means that the cash flow benefit of the first year's capital allowances occurs in year 1, as shown in line (g).
3. It has been assumed that the business as a whole is profit making and therefore it will pay the extra tax and be able to obtain the benefit of capital allowances on the normal timing.

the beginning of the project, account must now be taken of any cash inflows that may arise on the termination of the project, together with any tax consequences.

One would also have to deal with any outflows on termination, such as decommissioning a nuclear power station, at this stage.

FIXED ASSETS

As mentioned earlier in this chapter on page 53, when an asset is disposed of the capital allowances or depreciation will normally be limited to the difference between the cost of the asset and any money realized on its sale. This may result in additional capital allowances being given to bring the total allowances up to that difference, or it may result in allowances already given being taken back.

If the assets are to be retained in the business for use in other areas, then it is the sale value that is foregone that is relevant. If the business did not have the assets then it would have had to spend money to acquire similar assets. This outlay is no longer required since the assets are already owned so the cash flows are greater to that extent.

WORKING CAPITAL

If the net cash investment included the provision of extra working capital, then that extra working capital will be released when the project comes to an end, and will result in positive cash flows. In real life, of course, the build up of extra working capital and its release may be spread over a number of years and this timing will have to be allowed for in the cash flows.

Example 4.6

Using the same data as that given in Example 4.5, let us now assume that the plant and machinery is expected to have a resale value of £40,000 at the end of the six years. Let us also assume that the management of AB plc have set a minimum rate of return criterion of 10 per cent, then the cash flows and the calculation of the net present value would be as in Table 4.2. The project has a positive net present value of £13,070 so the project meets the criterion rate of return of 10 per cent. The profitability index would be 213,070/200,000 = 1.066.

COMPARISON OF BOOK VALUES AND CASH FLOWS

As stated previously, the cash flow totals will equal the values taken into the books of account, the only difference between the two being the timing of the different values. Using the data for the last example, the cash flow values and book values are compared in Table 4.3. In order to see how an increase in working capital is dealt with let us look at a further example.

Table 4.2 Example 4.6: cash flow table and calculation of NPV

Year	0	1	2	3	4	5	6	7	8
(a) Investment	-200.00								
(b) Operating cash flows		40.00	50.00	60.00	60.00	50.00	40.00		
(c) Tax at 35%			-14.00	-17.50	-21.00	-21.00	-17.50	-14.00	-4.66
'Pool' a/c:									
(d) *Added to pool*	*200.00*	*-37.50*	*-28.13*	*-21.09*	*-15.82*	*-11.87*	*-8.90*	*+13.30*	
(e) *Capital allowances*	*-50.00*	*112.50*	*84.38*	*63.28*	*47.46*	*35.60*	*26.70*	*Nil*	
(f) *Pool balance*	*150.00*								
(g) Tax saved		17.50	13.13	9.84	7.38	5.54	4.15	3.11	
(h) Sale of plant								40.00	
Annual cash flow	-200.00	57.50	49.13	52.34	46.38	34.54	26.65	29.11	-4.66
Present value factors 10%	1.00	0.909	0.826	0.751	0.683	0.621	0.564	0.513	0.467
Present values	-200.00	52.27	40.58	39.31	31.68	21.45	15.03	14.93	-2.18

Net present value = £13,070

Notes:

1. Line (e) has now changed because we are taking into account the £40,000 resale value of the plant. The pool account value for the assets at the end of year 6 is £26,700. It is sold for £40,000, so £13,300 of the capital allowances are taken back in year 7 giving the reversal in value for that year.

2. The sale value of the plant is a positive cash flow in year 7 at line (h) (different timing assumptions could have been made, i.e. take it in year 6).

3. The claw back of capital allowances in year 7 will reduce future capital allowances. This effect on cash flows has been taken in year 8. It would be reasonable to take these in year 7 as well. The present value at year 7 is 2.39 against the present value at year 8 of 2.18, so it has little effect on the outcome.

Table 4.3 Example 4.6: comparison of book values and cash flows

Totals used in cash flow			Totals recorded in accounts	
		£000s		£000s
Net profit before depreciation		300	Profit:	
Tax at 35%		−105	Before depreciation	300
			Depreciation (200 − 40)	−160
		195		
Capital allowances				140
(200 − 40)	160		Tax @ 35%	− 49
Tax @ 35% on 160		56		
			After tax profit	91
		251		
Cash received from			Cash flows shown by the	
sale of plant		40	accounts:	
			After-tax profit	91
			Depreciation	160
			Sale of plant	40
		291		291

Example 4.7

Leese and Williams plc have developed a new product and now propose to launch this product on the market. The proposal being looked at by the board of directors would involve the investment in plant and equipment of £500,000, £200,000 of which would be spent in the first year of construction and £300,000 being spent in the second year. The new product is expected to generate additional operating cash flows of £60,000 per year, and the divisional management concerned with the new product think that a return of £60,000 on the investment of £500,000 is adequate.

Further enquiries have been made and the following information must be considered. The new product would increase working capital by £60,000 in the first year in which it is operational, and a further £40,000 in the second year. The product is expected to have a life of 15 years at the end of which the plant would have a scrap value of £15,000. The extra working capital would be released in the last year of the product's life.

The tax rate is 35 per cent and capital allowances can be claimed at 25 per cent on the reducing balance basis. The board of directors has set a criterion rate of 10 per cent. The cash flows and the net present value can be calculated as in Table 4.4.

As can be seen from this example, the years for purchasing and commissioning of the plant have been designated year 0 and year 1 (alternatively

Table 4.4 Example 4.7: cash flow table and calculation of NPV

£000s

Year	0	1	2	3	4	5	6	7	8	9	10	11	12	13	14	15	16	17	18
Investment	-200.00	-300.00	—	—	—	—	—	—	—	—	—	—	—	—	—	—	—	—	—
Operating cash flows	—	—	60.00	60.00	60.00	60.00	60.00	60.00	60.00	60.00	60.00	60.00	60.00	60.00	60.00	60.00	60.00	—	—
Tax at 35%	—	—	—	-21.00	-21.00	-21.00	-21.00	-21.00	-21.00	-21.00	-21.00	-21.00	-21.00	-21.00	-21.00	-21.00	-21.00	-21.00	—
Pool a/c:																			
Added to pool	*500.00*	—	—	—	—	—	—	—	—	—	—	—	—	—	—	—	—	—	—
Capital allowances	*-125.00*	*-93.75*	*-70.31*	*-52.74*	*-39.55*	*-29.66*	*-22.25*	*-16.69*	*-12.51*	*-9.39*	*-7.04*	*-5.28*	*-3.96*	*-2.97*	*-2.23*	*-1.67*	*+9.99*	—	—
Pool balance	*375.00*	*281.25*	*210.94*	*158.20*	*118.65*	*88.99*	*66.74*	*50.06*	*37.54*	*28.16*	*21.12*	*15.84*	*11.88*	*8.91*	*6.68*	*5.01*	*Nil*	—	—
Tax saved by capital allowances	—	—	43.75	32.81	24.61	18.46	13.84	10.38	7.79	5.84	4.38	3.28	2.46	1.85	1.39	1.04	0.78	0.58	-3.50
Sale of plant	—	—	—	—	—	—	—	—	—	—	—	—	—	—	—	—	—	15.00	—
Working capital	—	—	-60.00	-40.00	—	—	—	—	—	—	—	—	—	—	—	—	100.00	—	—
Cash flow	-200.00	-300.00	43.75	31.81	63.61	57.46	52.84	49.38	46.79	44.84	43.38	42.28	41.46	40.85	40.39	40.04	139.78	-5.42	-3.50
PV factors 10%	1.000	0.909	0.826	0.751	0.683	0.621	0.564	0.513	0.467	0.424	0.386	0.350	0.319	0.290	0.263	0.239	0.218	0.198	0.180
Present value	-200.00	-272.70	36.14	23.89	43.45	35.68	29.80	25.33	21.85	19.01	16.74	14.80	13.23	11.85	10.62	9.57	30.47	-1.07	-0.63

Net present value = -130,970

the two years could have been designated year −1 and year 0, in which case the numbering of the other years would have been affected). The working capital requirement has been shown as a cash outflow in years 2 and 3, and at the end of the project in year 16 that cash is released and becomes a positive cash flow. There is a negative net present value which means that the project does not meet the required rate of return of 10 per cent.

DIMINISHING INFLUENCE OF LATER YEARS

It has already been mentioned that values most distant in time have the least effect on the project and this is evident in the last illustration. In the later years of the project the low PV factors reduce the values to relatively insignificant figures—the further away in time the greater that effect. Of course the further away in time that events occur the more difficult they are to forecast. One benefit of DCF is that it does reduce the influence of those distant events on the outcome of the appraisal.

MORE THAN ONE DCF SOLUTION

A project being evaluated may be one that has substantial future *negative* cash flows. This can arise where there are planned expansions to the project, or there are large costs involved at the end of the project to restore the site used because of environmental requirements. In such cases it is possible for there to be more than one outcome of the appraisal process. This is shown in the following calculations.

1. *Project*: Investment £150.
   Cash flows: Year 1 £100, Year 2 £100, Year 3 £100, Year 4 £100, Year 5 £−270.
   Cost of capital: 8 per cent.
2. *Present value of cash flows*: These are given in Table 4.5.
3. Starting with the last year bring back the negative cash flows year by year, at the cost of capital to the business, until a year is reached when the value is positive:

Year 5 −270/1.08 = −250	+ Year 4 100 = −150 (value still negative)
Year 4 −150/1.08 = −139	+ Year 3 100 = − 39 (value still negative)
Year 3 − 39/1.08 = − 36	+ Year 2 100 = 64 (this is now a positive figure)

4. The DCF calculation then appears as in Table 4.6.

Table 4.5 Present value of cash flows

Year	Cash flow £000s	PV factor for 10%	Present value £000s	PV factor for 26%	Present value £000s
1	100	0.909	91	0.794	79
2	100	0.826	83	0.630	63
3	100	0.751	75	0.500	50
4	100	0.683	68	0.397	40
5	−270	0.621	−168	0.315	−85
			149		147

Table 4.6 DCF calculation

Year	Cash flow £000s	PV factor for 7%	Present value £000s
1	100	0.935	94
2	64	0.873	56
			150

One way to resolve the problem is to use the present value method to see if the project meets the criterion rate, and then to rank the project by the profitability index. Alternatively the most distant negative cash flows could be reduced by the cost of capital year by year in the way shown in point 3 on page 63 and Tables 4.5 and 4.6 above.

It must be emphasized that such situations are extremely rare and only occur where there are very substantial negative cash outflows in distant time periods.

5. DCF problems and solutions

In order to give a wider view of the range of decisions that may be required in practice, this chapter looks at a series of simulated problems and their solutions. While people beginning to use DCF may have a grasp of the essentials there are often problems when they try to put the ideas into practice. The problems set out here are designed to give the reader a chance to apply the theory that has been dealt with so far in a more realistic way.

The layout of the cash flow calculations used in this book is one that is most likely to be found in practice. There are, however, other ways in which the data can be displayed, such as setting out the net cash investment, the annual cash flows and the residual values separately.

Stages in the solution

When appraising any capital investment problem the key question that needs to be answered is: 'Will the cash flows that are forecast to arise from the project provide an adequate rate of return on the funds locked up in that investment?'

NET PRESENT VALUE METHOD
When using this method the steps required to find the solution are:

1. Management must fix the criterion rate, or rates, of return. Ideally this should be done as part of the long-term planning for the business. A single rate may be used, or, if appropriate, several rates may be set for different risk categories.
2. Ascertain what the net change in the firm's cash position will be if the firm goes ahead with the investment. This measurement must take into account *all* the cash flow consequences including inflows from assets disposed of.
3. Estimate the operating cash flows that are expected year by year during the life of the project, allocating them to the years in which they are expected to arise. These include:
   (a) extra profit before depreciation resulting from the investment;
   (b) any tax payable in those increased profits;
   (c) look at the tax relief given by the effect of capital allowances or depreciation. In many cases timing differences will preclude these being set off against the profit before depreciation so it is unlikely that tax can be calculated on the net profit as a single figure;
   (d) what cash flows will arise when the project ends and assets are disposed of, together with any tax consequences.

4. Find the present value of the future cash flows by discounting them by the criterion rate, using the table in Appendix A or B.

5. If the sum of all the present values is a positive figure the project has a rate of return greater than the criterion rate and is therefore acceptable. If it is a negative figure then the project does not meet the criterion rate and is not acceptable.

6. When the project is acceptable then it should be ranked with other projects by calculating the profitability index.

DCF OR INTERNAL RATE OF RETURN (IRR)
When using this method the steps to be followed are:

1. Calculate the net cash investment and annual and residual cash flows as in 2 and 3 above.

2. Find the discount rate that will produce as near a zero figure as possible for the present value of *all* of the cash flows. This discount rate is the DCF rate of return or IRR.

Exercise 5.1
As the office manager of BG plc you are in the process of preparing a proposal to put to the board of directors for the installation of new computer equipment at a cost of £28,000. The data processing methods used to date are less efficient than those currently available and if replaced by the new equipment should produce cost savings (before depreciation) of £5,000 per year. The committee that vets all investment proposals requires the submissions to show a rate of return of at least 10 per cent for the project.

The new equipment is expected to have a life of eight years, after which it would have a residual value of £4,000. The rate of corporation tax is 35 per cent and capital allowances can be claimed at 25 per cent on the reducing balance.

The solution is given in Table 5.1. As this present value is a minus figure it means that the project does not meet the criterion rate of 10 per cent and should not be approved.

Exercise 5.2
As the chief executive of a subsidiary within a group of companies which operates in an overseas territory which was formerly a French colony, you are formulating a proposal to put before the main board for the replacement of a kiln with a more modern electric version. The present kiln will be disposed of and there has been an offer to purchase it for 60,000 francs, which would exactly match the written-down value for tax purposes. The new kiln will cost Fr800,000 exclusive of VAT and have an effective life of eight years, after which it is expected to realize Fr50,000. Your cost department

66

Table 5.1

Year	0	1	2	3	4	5	6	7	8	9	10
Investment	-28,000										
Operating cash flow		5,000	5,000	5,000	5,000	5,000	5,000	5,000	5,000		
Tax @ 35%			-1,750	-1,750	-1,750	-1,750	-1,750	-1,750	-1,750	-1,750	-1,750
Pool a/c:											
Added	*28,000*										
Capital allowance	*-7,000*	*-5,250*	*-3,938*	*-2,953*	*-2,215*	*-1,661*	*-1,246*	*-934*	*-701*	*+1,898*	
Balance	*21,000*	*15,750*	*11,813*	*8,859*	*6,645*	*4,983*	*3,738*	*2,803*	*2,102*	*Nil*	
Tax saved		2,450	1,838	1,378	1,034	775	581	436	327	245	-664
Sale of equipment										4,000	
Cash flow	-28,000	7,450	5,088	4,628	4,284	4,025	3,831	3,686	3,577	2,495	-664
PV factors 10%	1.000	0.909	0.826	0.751	0.683	0.621	0.564	0.513	0.467	0.424	0.386
Present value	-28,000	6,772	4,202	3,476	2,926	2,500	2,161	1,891	1,670	1,058	-256
Net present value	£-1,600										

67

estimates that the new kiln will save operating costs of Fr240,000 before depreciation.

Tax on companies (*impôt sur les sociétés*) is currently at the rate of 50 per cent and is assessed partly on a 'pay as you earn' basis, with four-fifths of the tax being paid on an estimated basis during the year in which profits are earned with the remainder payable during the following year. Depreciation allowances (*amortissement*) can be provided at 10 per cent of cost on a straight line basis from the year in which the plant is fully put into use, which in this case would be the first full year the kiln is operational. Where depreciable plant is disposed of, any gain or loss on the written-down value is taken as a short-term gain or loss, taxed at the normal tax rate for companies.

The main board require the proposals for all new investments to show the internal rate of return. The calculations for this are shown in Table 5.2. The net present value using a discount rate of 15 per cent is +Fr16,700 so the IRR is above 15 per cent (and is in fact 15.6).

Exercise 5.3

You are preparing to take out a single premium life insurance policy for an annual premium of £2,000. From the details that have been quoted you estimate that at the end of the fifteen years' currency of the policy it would realize, including bonuses, the sum of £63,650. Before committing yourself to this investment you would like to know the rate of return that you would earn on the money you would be putting into the policy, assuming that you survive the full fifteen years.

1. Negative cash flows in years 1 to 15: £2,000
    = a present value of $2,000 \times 7.606$ (PV factor for 10% years 1–15) = £15,212
2. Positive cash flow in year 15:
    = $63,650 \times 0.239$ (PV factor for 10%) = £15,212

The return that would be earned is therefore 10 per cent.

Exercise 5.4

(a) You have been asked to advise a company that has recently negotiated a licensing agreement with a US corporation that will enable it to manufacture and sell a new product in addition to the company's existing product line. The manager for the new product line and his staff have been investigating the problems of manufacturing and selling the product with a view to gaining board sanction for the necessary capital expenditure.

It is estimated that the product would sell for £60 per unit, and the variable costs associated with its manufacture and sale would be £30 per unit. The new product would incur extra fixed overheads of £5 million per year (including £500,000 depreciation). The product manager and his

Table 5.2

Year	0 Fr000s	1 Fr000s	2 Fr000s	3 Fr000s	4 Fr000s	5 Fr000s	6 Fr000s	7 Fr000s	8 Fr000s	9 Fr000s	10 Fr000s
Cost of kiln	-800										
Sale of old kiln	60										
Operating cash flow		240	240	240	240	240	240	240	240	—	
Depreciation allowance		-80	-80	-80	-80	-80	-80	-80	-80	-110	
Net profit		160	160	160	160	160	160	160	160	-110	
Tax @ 50%		-64	-80	-80	-80	-80	-80	-80	-80	28	11
Sale of kiln										50	
Cash flow	-740	176	160	160	160	160	160	160	160	78	11
PV factors 15%	1.000	0.870				3.617[1]				0.284	0.247
Present value	-740	153.1				578.7				22.2	2.7

NPV @ 15% = Fr16,700

1. Appendix B: Year 8 – Year 1 = 4.487 – 0.870

Notes:

1. As there is no difference in the timing of the operating cash flows and the claiming of depreciation, they can be netted off against each other and the tax calculated on the net profit.

2. Four-fifths of the tax on the first year's profits is paid in that year, the balance in the following year. This leaves a tax payment of Fr16,000 in year 9 against which is offset the four-fifths of the tax relief of Fr55,000 on the additional depreciation allowances of Fr110,000 given in that year, with the balance of the extra tax relief being given in year 10.

3. As the cash flows for years 2 to 8 are equal, instead of working out each year's present value individually, it can be done in one calculation using Appendix B. Take the PV factor for 15 per cent for years 1 to 8, and then delete the present value for the year that is not required, in this case year 1.

team have already spent £250,000 investigating the product and its market and drawing up the proposals. It is estimated that the company would be able to sell 200,000 units per year. The fixed and variable costs include the licensing costs of a fixed fee and annual royalty.

New plant and machinery would be required at a cost of £6 million, and extra working capital would be required of £1.5 million spread over the year of commissioning the plant and the first year of its operational use. The foreseeable life of the project is twelve years, and at the end of that period the plant and machinery would have a scrap value of £100,000. The current rate of corporation tax is 35 per cent.

The board requires a minimum rate of return on new investments of 10 per cent.

The calculations are given in Table 5.3. On the basis of the 10 per cent discount rate used we are left with a positive present value of £1.48 million, and the project as such is viable, given the criterion rate set. Its profitability index is £8.98m/7.5 = 1.107. (The present value of the annual and residual values must be about £8.98, because there is a net present value of £1.48 after deduction of the total investment of plant £6m plus working capital of £1.5m.)

(b) The board have examined the proposals submitted to them and, in view of the low profitability index, have asked for a reappraisal of the project on the basis that the sales volume will only reach 180,000 units per year. At this level of turnover the additional working capital required would only be £1.2 million.

The calculations for this are given in Table 5.4. In this case the net present value is a negative figure, so the project as stated would not meet the criterion rate of return. The board would now have to make a judgement as to the probability of the volume falling as low as 180,000 units. If it was at all likely then the project should not be approved.

Exercise 5.5

You manage a retail outlet for a major motor vehicle distributor in Kuwait. You are having some difficulty in persuading the board of the company that you work for to spend 150,000 dinars on a new canopy and air-conditioning for your forecourt and showroom which would have an expected life of ten years. The average profit made per car sold is 400 dinars.

The company requires a minimum rate of return of 15 per cent on all new investments. There is no corporate tax in Kuwait.

How may extra cars would you have to sell per year to meet this rate of return requirement?

Present value factor for 15 per cent for 1 dinar per year for each of years 1 to 10 is 5.019 (from Appendix B). Simply divide this factor into the

Table 5.3

Year	0 £m	1 £m	2 £m	3 £m	4 £m	5 £m	6 £m	7 £m	8 £m	9 £m	10 £m	11 £m	12 £m	13 £m	14 £m
Cost of plant	-6.00														
Operating cash flow[1]		1.50	1.50	1.50	1.50	1.50	1.50	1.50	1.50	1.50	1.50	1.50	1.50		
Tax @ 35%			-0.53	-0.53	-0.53	-0.53	-0.53	-0.53	-0.53	-0.53	-0.53	-0.53	-0.53	-0.53	
Pool a/c:															
Added	*6.00*														
Capital allowance	*-1.50*	*-1.13*	*-0.84*	*-0.63*	*-0.47*	*-0.36*	*-0.27*	*-0.21*	*-0.15*	*-0.11*	*-0.08*	*-0.06*	*-0.05*	*-0.04*	
Balance	*4.50*	*3.38*	*2.53*	*1.90*	*1.42*	*1.07*	*0.80*	*0.60*	*0.45*	*0.34*	*0.25*	*0.19*	*0.14*		*0.01*
Tax saved		0.53	0.39	0.30	0.22	0.17	0.12	0.09	0.07	0.05	0.04	0.03	0.02	0.02	0.01
Working capital	-0.75	-0.75											1.50		
Sale of plant														0.10	
Cash flow	-6.75	1.28	1.36	1.27	1.19	1.14	1.09	1.06	1.04	1.02	1.01	1.00	2.49	-0.41	0.01
PV factors 10%	1.000	0.909	0.826	0.751	0.683	0.621	0.564	0.513	0.467	0.424	0.386	0.350	0.319	0.290	0.263
Present value	-6.75	1.16	1.13	0.95	0.81	0.71	0.61	0.54	0.49	0.43	0.39	0.35	0.79	-0.12	0

Net present value @ 10% = £1,480,000

1. (SP 60 – VC 30)200,000 – FC of £4.5 million (£5m less £0.5m depreciation).
2. It should be noted that the £250,000 already spent on the product has not been taken into account as this is a sunk cost and will remain whether or not the board decide to proceed with the project.

Table 5.4

Year	0	1	2	3	4	5	6	7	8	9	10	11	12	13	14
	£m	£m	£m	£m	£m	£m	£m	£m	£m	£m	£m	£m	£m	£m	£m
Cost of plant	-6.00														
Operating cash flow		0.90	0.90	0.90	0.90	0.90	0.90	0.90	0.90	0.90	0.90	0.90	0.90		
Tax @ 35%			-0.32	-0.32	-0.32	-0.32	-0.32	-0.32	-0.32	-0.32	-0.32	-0.32	-0.32	-0.32	
Pool a/c:															
Added	*6.00*														
Capital allowances	*-1.50*	*-1.13*	*-0.84*	*-0.63*	*-0.47*	*-0.36*	*-0.27*	*-0.20*	*-0.15*	*-0.11*	*-0.08*	*-0.06*	*-0.05*	*-0.04*	
Balance	*4.50*	*3.38*	*2.53*	*1.90*	*1.42*	*1.07*	*0.80*	*0.60*	*0.45*	*0.34*	*0.25*	*0.19*	*0.14*	*Nil*	
Tax saved		0.53	0.39	0.30	0.22	0.17	0.12	0.09	0.07	0.05	0.04	0.03	0.02	0.02	0.01
Working capital	-0.60	-0.60											1.2	0.10	
Sale of plant															
Cash flow	-6.60	0.83	0.97	0.88	0.80	0.75	0.70	0.68	0.65	0.63	0.62	0.61	1.80	-0.20	0.01
PV factors 10%	1.000	0.909	0.826	0.751	0.683	0.621	0.564	0.513	0.467	0.424	0.386	0.350	0.319	0.290	0.263
Present value	-6.60	0.75	0.80	0.66	0.55	0.47	0.39	0.34	0.30	0.27	0.24	0.21	0.57	-0.06	0

Net present value @ 10% = -£1.11

investment to give the annual cash flow that must be achieved to meet the required rate of return:

$$150,000/5.019 = 29,886 \text{ dinars per year}$$

This means that the manager would have to sell an extra 74 cars per year, i.e. $29,886/400 = 74$.

Exercise 5.6

The board of Forkson & Co. Ltd. are considering launching a new product which they hope will restore the profitability of their company. In recent years the business has only just broken even in trading in its existing products, and there is no immediate prospect that profitability can be restored on the existing products.

The new product would require the expenditure of £80,000 on new plant, and £20,000 on removal and retraining costs which will be refunded by the development agency one year later. It is estimated that the product will have a life of eight years after which it will probably be replaced by a new line. The plant would be scrapped and is likely to realize £12,400 on disposal. The extra profit before depreciation is expected to be £14,000 in year 1, £16,000 in year 2, £18,000 in each of years 3 to 5, £16,000 in year 6, £15,000 in year 7, and £10,000 in year 8. Additional working capital would be required in the year prior to sales commencing of £8,000 with an additional £10,000 being required in the following year. This is expected to be released in the last year of sales.

Looking at the company's overall tax position its past losses mean that any tax is not likely to be paid until year 3 of the project. Because of the low level of profit the company will only pay corporation tax at 25 per cent, the small company rate.

Before considering the matter further the board want to know whether the rate of return earned on the investment would exceed 9 per cent.

The calculations to solve this problem are given in Table 5.5. Note that the benefit of capital allowances and the taxation on the extra profit have both been deferred until the company actually expects to make tax payments.

Exercise 5.7

A medium-sized spring-making company STL plc is proposing to expand its operations by purchasing an automatic coil-winding machine for £500,000. Delivery of the new machine would take place half way through the company's current year and it would contribute to that year's profits. An additional £10,000 working capital would be required due to the expansion of the business.

The machine is being acquired in an overseas territory whose government

73

Table 5.5

Year	0 £000s	1 £000s	2 £000s	3 £000s	4 £000s	5 £000s	6 £000s	7 £000s	8 £000s	9 £000s	10 £000s
Investment	-80.0										
Removal costs etc.	-20.0	20.0									
Operating cash flow		14.0	16.0	18.0	18.0	18.0	16.0	15.0	10.0	-2.5	
Tax @ 25%				-7.5	-4.5	-4.5	-4.5	-4.0	-3.8		
Pool a/c:											
Added	80.0										
Capital allowances	-20.0	-15.0	-11.3	-8.4	-6.3	-4.7	-3.6	-2.7	+4.4		
Balance	60.00	45.0	33.8	25.3	19.0	14.2	10.7	8.0	Nil		
Tax saved					2.1	1.6	1.2	0.9	0.7	-1.1	
Working capital	-8.0	-10.0		11.6					18.0		
Sale of plant									12.4		
Cash flow	-108.0	24.0	16.0	22.1	15.6	15.1	12.7	11.9	37.3	-3.6	
PV factors 9%	1.000	0.917	0.842	0.772	0.708	0.650	0.596	0.547	0.502	0.460	
Present value	-108.0	22.0	13.5	17.1	11.1	9.8	7.6	6.5	18.7	-1.7	

NPV = -£3,400

agencies provide a 45 per cent grant towards the cost of the new machine which is likely to take a year to process. The balance of the cost is allowed in the form of a depreciation allowance of 20 per cent of the reducing balance.

It is proposed that the machine would be disposed of five years after the end of the current year, when it would have a second-hand value of £6,000. The increase in profit before depreciation is expected to be £50,000 in the year in which the machine is installed and £120,000 per annum for each of the next five years.

The company's criterion rate of return is 8 per cent after tax. The current tax rate in the territory is 40 per cent. The solution is given in Table 5.6. In this case, as the timing of the earning of profits and claiming depreciation allowances are the same, the tax can be calculated on the net profit.

Exercise 5.8

Capont plc is currently considering the manufacture and sale of a new product, Brando, in order to supplement its existing product range. In order to put Brando onto the market an investment of £650,000 in plant and machinery would be required. In addition there would be an increase in the amount invested in working capital which is expected to amount to £140,000 in the year in which the assets are required, and a further £50,000 the following year.

The new product is expected to increase profits before depreciation by £180,000 per year for years 1 to 8, £100,000 p.a. in years 9 and 10, and £80,000 in year 11, this being the expected life of the product. As the product's life draws to an end the additional working capital will be released amounting to £60,000 in year 11 and £130,000 the following year. In that year the plant would be scrapped to realize an expected £29,000.

The current tax rate is 35 per cent and normal capital allowances will be claimed. The board of directors have set a minimum acceptable rate of return of 10 per cent, and also, especially for high-risk projects like the above, require the internal rate of return to be calculated.

The relevant calculations are given in Table 5.7, and from this data it can be seen that the project comfortably exceeds the criterion rate, and that the IRR must be about 13.5 per cent.

Exercise 5.9

A highway authority is evaluating the cost effectiveness of different types of highway construction. For new highways, varying types of construction can be used, each of which has a different initial cost level, and a different pattern of maintenance.

In considering its long-term commitments for both new construction and maintenance, the authority wishes to take into account the cost of the funds that are needed to finance the work.

75

Table 5.6

Year	0 £000s	1 £000s	2 £000s	3 £000s	4 £000s	5 £000s	6 £000s	7 £000s
Cost of machine	-500.0							
Grant received		225.0						
Depreciation:								
Net cost	275.0							
Annual depreciation	-55.0	-44.0	-35.2	-28.2	-22.5	-18.0	-66.1	
Balance	220.0	176.0	140.8	112.6	90.1	72.1	Nil	
Profit before depreciation	50.0	120.0	120.0	120.0	120.0	120.0		
Depreciation	-55.0	-44.0	-35.2	-28.2	-22.5	-18.0		
Profit after depreciation	-5.0	76.0	84.8	91.8	97.5	102.0		
Tax @ 40%		2.0	-30.4	-33.9	-36.7	-39.0	-40.8	
Working capital	-10.0					10.0		
Sale of machine							6.0	26.4*
Cash flow	-460.0	347.0	89.6	86.1	83.3	91.0	-34.8	26.4
PV factors 8%	1.000	0.926	0.857	0.794	0.735	0.681	0.630	0.583
Present value at 8%	-460.0	321.3	76.8	68.3	61.2	62.0	-21.9	15.4
Net present value = £123,100								

*This is the tax rate on the additional depreciation allowances of £66,100 on disposal of the machine.

76

Table 5.7

Year	0 £000s	1 £000s	2 £000s	3 £000s	4 £000s	5 £000s	6 £000s	7 £000s	8 £000s	9 £000s	10 £000s	11 £000s	12 £000s	13 £000s
Cost of plant	-650.0													
Working capital	-140.0	-50.0										60.0	130.0	
Operating cash flow		180.0	180.0	180.0	180.0	180.0	180.0	180.0	180.0	100.0	100.0	80.0		
Tax at 35%			-63.0	-63.0	-63.0	-63.0	-63.0	-63.0	-63.0	-63.0	-35.0	-35.0	-28.0	
Pool a/c:														
Added	*650.0*													
Capital allowances	*-162.5*	*-121.9*	*-91.4*	*-68.6*	*-51.4*	*-38.6*	*-28.9*	*-21.7*	*-16.3*	*-12.2*	*-9.2*	*-6.9*	*+8.4*	*-2.9*
Balance	*487.5*	*365.6*	*274.2*	*205.7*	*154.2*	*115.7*	*86.8*	*65.1*	*48.8*	*36.6*	*27.5*	*20.6*	*Nil*	
Tax saved		56.9	42.7	32.0	24.0	18.0	13.5	10.1	7.6	5.7	4.3	3.2	2.4	-2.9
Sale of plant													29.0	
Cash flow	-790.0	186.9	159.7	149.0	141.0	135.0	130.5	127.1	124.6	42.7	69.3	108.2	133.4	-2.9
PV factors 10%	1.000	0.909	0.826	0.751	0.683	0.621	0.564	0.513	0.467	0.424	0.386	0.350	0.319	0.290
Present value @ 10%	-790.0	169.9	131.9	111.9	96.3	83.8	73.6	65.2	58.2	18.1	26.7	37.9	39.7	-0.8

Net present value at 10% = £122,400 (profitability index 962.4/840.0 = 1.15)

Net present value @ 12% = £50.4
Net present value @ 14% = -£12.4
Net present value @ 13% = £17.9

The information that has been supplied to the authority by its consulting engineers regarding the possible cost levels for differing types of construction, and the consequent maintenance commitments, are as follows:

	£000s per route mile
Method A: Initial cost	3,500
Maintenance costs every three years	500
Method B: Initial cost	4,150
Maintenance costs every five years	520
Method C: Initial cost	4,820
Maintenance costs every eight years	550

The Treasurer's Department estimates the likely future costs of borrowing over the foreseeable future will be 6 per cent.

You have been asked to advise the authority, on the basis of the above information, the form of construction that is the most economical over an estimated forty-year life.

The solution to this problem can best be approached by considering the total construction and maintenance costs over the expected life of the highway. The method of construction that would have the least overall present value of those costs, discounted at the cost of borrowing to the authority, is the most desirable in financial terms. The calculations for the three methods are given in Tables 5.8, 5.9 and 5.10.

Table 5.8 Construction Method A

Year	Outlays £000s	PV factors for 6%	Present value of outlays £000s
0	3,500	1.000	3,500
3	500	0.840	
6	500	0.705	
9	500	0.592	
12	500	0.497	
15	500	0.417	
18	500	0.350	Total = 4.695 → 2,347
21	500	0.294	
24	500	0.247	
27	500	0.207	
30	500	0.174	
33	500	0.146	
36	500	0.123	
39	500	0.103	
Total	10,000		5,847

Table 5.9 Construction Method B

Year	Outlays £000s	PV Factors for 6%		Present value of outlays £000s
0	4,150	1.000		4,150
5	520	0.747		
10	520	0.558		
15	520	0.417		
20	520	0.312	Total = 2.668	1,387
25	520	0.233		
30	520	0.174		
35	520	0.130		
40	520	0.097		
Total	8,310			5,537

Table 5.10 Construction Method C

Year	Outlays £000s	PV Factors for 6%		Present value of outlay £000s
0	4,820	1.000		4,820
8	550	0.627		
18	550	0.394	Total = 1.520	836
24	550	0.247		
32	550	0.155		
40	550	0.097		
Total	7,570			5,656

From the point of view of the highway authority, Method B would be the most advantageous, since it has the lowest present value of costs. The above analysis might well be expanded, however, to take into account differences in social costs due to the varying frequency and duration of the highway being wholly or partially out of service. This could well be incorporated into the calculations previously made if the data is available. If not, then it should still be a factor that should be taken into account in some way in the decision.

Section 3

Use of DCF in specific areas

6. *Alternative choice problems and leasing versus buying*

Once management has made a decision to go ahead with a particular project, for example a new product launch, or cost saving via more automation, it may find that there is more than one way in which that objective can be achieved. Where there are a number of viable alternatives then further thought must be given to which of those alternatives is the best from the point of view of the rate of return that it can earn compared with the other alternatives. These alternatives may be related to the way in which the project itself is to be organized, e.g. particular machines, methods of production, marketing strategy, etc., or they may be concerned with how the use of the assets that are required is to be obtained, e.g. by outright purchase, leasing, and so on. The first part of this chapter is concerned with the alternative ways of organizing the project itself, and the second part with the specific aspect of leasing versus buying.

Alternative choice problems

IMPORTANCE OF SEEKING ALTERNATIVES
When formulating a project it is important that all methods of achieving the objectives of that project are thoroughly explored and appraised. Often only cursory thought is given to alternatives when a project is drawn up, and while that original proposal may meet the minimum rate of return criteria, it is possible that other ways of carrying out the project may affect either or both the rate of return on the project and the overall rate of return on capital employed for the business. Bearing in mind the effect that the project profitability has on the overall level of profitability of the company, management must continuously search for alternative ways of achieving objectives that will raise the general level of profitability of the firm. The appropriate place for this search for alternatives is at the planning stage for projects, before they are approved and money committed to them.

The funds available to a business must, in most cases, be looked upon as a scarce resource from which the maximum benefit must be derived. Each proposal to spend money on a particular use should be looked upon in this light. The allocation of money to one purpose necessarily means that alternative and competing projects cannot be proceeded with. The cost of any project is then, in a sense, the return that could have been earned on those competing projects had they not been dropped to enable that one to proceed.

When investigating the alternative ways of carrying out a project the critical elements that must be considered are:

1. the amount of money that has to be invested;
2. the increase in operating cash flows, and therefore profits, that are expected;
3. the differential tax effects.

The successful management is the one that consistently selects the right combination of these factors within its overall portfolio of activities and so produces a higher than average rate of return.

The consideration of alternatives is something that should be built into the appraisal process and be required by those whose function it is to approve or reject projects. Profitability is not about the absolute level of profit, but how much profit is earned in relation to the capital that has to be invested to earn it. It reinforces the need for long-term decision-making to be made at the top and not left to line managers. The latter may tend to view the need to maximize profits as the main requirement for investment within their area of responsibility, without fully considering the level of investment that is required to achieve that profit, or for the profitability requirement for the business as a whole.

ECONOMY IN THE USE OF FUNDS

Optimizing the use of funds will materially help in maximizing the return on capital employed. The investment of £2 million on a project that will produce an operating cash flow of £400,000 per year is likely to be more profitable than an investment of £3.5 million on a more sophisticated version of the same project that will produce an operating cash flow of £550,000. The investment of £3.5 million, considered on its own, may well satisfy the minimum rate of return criteria, and therefore be an acceptable project. But if management is aware of the alternative investment of £2 million, it can then consider whether the incremental investment of £1.5 million to achieve the more sophisticated version gives an incremental operating cash flow that provides a return greater than what could be achieved by investing that £1.5 million in other projects.

When considering a project similar to that just outlined, management should have before it a statement of the rate of return on the basic project together with rates of return on the incremental investments needed to reach the more sophisticated versions of the same project. These incremental investments and the related returns can then be considered in the ranking process to see whether or not the incremental investment could earn a higher return if used to invest in other projects. If it can earn a higher rate of return than could be earned on other projects then the more sophisticated version of the project with its higher investment would be adopted. If not then the more basic version of the project should be adopted and the incremental investment used to finance a higher yielding project.

Economy in the use of funds does not necessarily mean that one is always looking for ways to *reduce* the amount of money invested in a project. The advantages of major automation projects, for example, which will drastically affect the cost structure of a business, can produce benefits from the advantages of scale, so the higher the investment the higher the return on the incremental investment. What we are concerned with is to ensure as far as possible that each £1 invested earns the highest rate of return achievable within the context of the long-term future of the business.

OPERATING CHOICES

There are a range of choices in the way in which the various operations of the business are carried out. The different combinations of materials, layout of plant and sequence of operations, marketing strategies, stock levels, etc., are typical of the factors that should be investigated at this stage. Once the business has acquired specific forms of fixed assets, the range of choices open to management is greatly restricted. The planning stage is the time when painless adjustments to the original plan can be made if detailed investigations reveal that this is desirable.

NON-OPERATING CHOICES

Quite apart from the detailed way in which a project will be carried out there will also be a range of external factors that must be considered. Various countries give grants or waive taxes for businesses that conform to specific requirements of location, levels of employment, etc. These can have a significant effect on the rate of return on a project. The unification of the EC into a single market means that a number of projects may have to be considered in a European framework rather than a national domestic framework, combining the various incentives that may be offered by governments with optimizing the impact that the single market may have on the outcome of a particular project.

Approach to alternative choice problems

Where there are a number of different ways of carrying out a project the identification of the optimum method should be approached logically. The volume of work involved can be substantially reduced by discarding at an early stage those alternatives that are clearly non-starters. This process of elimination can be based upon normal forecasting techniques during the preparation of the basic data. Once the clearly less profitable alternatives are discarded those that remain should be arranged in a logical sequence.

A useful scheme for solving multiple-choice problems is given below. This sequence starts, as should all our thinking, with setting out the objective of the project and what it is trying to achieve.

1. Analyse and define the objective of the proposal.
2. Set out the possible alternative methods of achieving that objective.
3. Drop any alternatives which, on the data already assembled, are non-starters.
4. Quantify all the consequences that would flow from each of the remaining alternatives.
5. Some of the consequences of alternatives may not be capable of being quantified, e.g. employee relationships. These must be evaluated in some way and taken into account in the final decision.
6. Weigh up all the factors in 4 and 5 above for each alternative and reach a decision.

NON-FINANCIAL DATA

It will be noted in 5 above that some factors cannot be evaluated in financial terms. This is likely to be the case in many business decisions, and it must be stressed that in those cases a decision cannot be made on financial criteria alone. The non-financial consequences of an investment decision may have far-reaching effects on the business and it would be quite wrong for these to be ignored. While the financial consequences, one hopes, will be fully evaluated, the fact that money values have been ascribed to them does not necessarily mean that they are the most important factors.

Obviously non-financial data cannot, by its nature, be incorporated into the DCF appraisal, and this means that there is a danger of it being ignored at the decision-taking stage. The attitude that insists that the financially measured data are the sole criteria on which a decision should be based should be guarded against, and management, in setting out the framework within which the processes of drawing up an investment proposal and its submission are made, should ensure that such factors are always spelt out.

SEQUENTIAL TREATMENT OF ALTERNATIVES

Once the alternatives that are to be evaluated have been defined, the next step is to quantify the consequences of each course of action. Each alternative could be evaluated as though it were a separate project without any reference to any of the other alternatives, and then the one that shows the highest rate of return would be selected. But, as has already been demonstrated, this might not be the best solution. The critical factor, as far as management is concerned, is the return on the *incremental* investment required between one alternative and another, by taking a step-by-step progression through the alternatives that are to be appraised. Starting with the alternative with the lowest investment one would work upwards through each incremental level, to the alternative with the highest investment. At each step the rate of return on the incremental investment should be calculated.

To do nothing is just as much a choice as any other alternative, and this has been recognized in the problems that have been looked at so far. The solution to these problems has been to compare the cash flow differences between doing nothing and carrying on as the business is presently constituted, or proceeding with an investment proposal that has been submitted to management for approval. What we are concerned with now is to take that comparison one step further and look at the cash flow differences between a series of alternatives for the same project. This is illustrated in the following example.

Example 6.1

The directors of Rose and Bloom plc are considering the renewal or replacement of the power plant for their main factory. This plant is fifteen years old and it is proposed that it should undergo modernization, including the installation of automated controls at a cost of £100,000. When complete the work should result in cost savings (before depreciation) in the order of £22,000 per year. The written-down value of the plant for tax purposes is £30,000, and if it were to be sold now it would realize approximately £5,000 as scrap. The renovation would give the plant a further useful life of ten years, at the end of which it would realize about the same amount as scrap.

After looking at the scheme in some detail, a further proposal has been formulated that would involve the complete replacement of the power plant by one incorporating all the latest fuel-saving devices. This would cost about £250,000, and would result in cost savings before depreciation of about £44,000 per year. It would have a useful life of fifteen years, at the end of which it should realize some £7,000 as scrap.

Management has set a rate of return criterion of 10 per cent for projects in the category comprising projects such as this one.

Stage 1

The first step in reaching a decision is to decide whether or not the least expensive alternative, in terms of cash outlay, would be a project which meets the criterion rate of return. This part of the decision-making process proceeds along the lines used in previous examples, and the calculations are laid out in Table 6.1.

As can be seen from the table the project has a positive NPV when the cash flows are discounted at 10 per cent so the project has a rate of return that exceeds the criterion and is acceptable. From the further calculations made it can also be seen that the actual rate of return is 15 per cent.

Stage 2

The appraisal of the alternative with the lower cash investment has shown that this would be an acceptable project. We must now turn our attention to the appraisal of the return that would be earned by investing the additional

Table 6.1

Year	0 £000s	1 £000s	2 £000s	3 £000s	4 £000s	5 £000s	6 £000s	7 £000s	8 £000s	9 £000s	10 £000s	11 £000s	12 £000s
Cost of renovating plant	-100.0												
Operating cash flow		22.0	22.0	22.0	22.0	22.0	22.0	22.0	22.0	22.0	22.0		
Tax at 35%		-7.7	-7.7	-7.7	-7.7	-7.7	-7.7	-7.7	-7.7	-7.7	-7.7	-7.7	
Pool a/c:													
Added	100.0												
Capital allowances	-25.0	-18.8	-14.1	-10.5	-7.9	-5.9	-4.4	-3.3	-2.5	-1.9	-1.4	+0.8	-0.3
Balance	75.0	56.3	42.2	31.6	23.7	17.8	13.3	10.0	7.5	5.6	4.2	—	
Tax saved @ 35%		8.8	6.6	4.9	3.7	2.8	2.1	1.6	1.2	0.9	0.7	0.5	-0.3
Scrap value of plant												5.0	
Cash flow	-100.0	30.8	20.9	19.2	18.0	17.1	16.4	15.9	15.5	15.2	15.0	-2.2	-0.3
PV factors 10%	1.000	0.909	0.826	0.751	0.683	0.621	0.564	0.513	0.467	0.424	0.386	0.350	0.319
Present value 10%	-100.0	28.0	17.3	14.4	12.3	10.6	9.2	8.2	7.2	6.4	5.8	-0.8	-0.1
NPV 10%	18.4												
NPV 12%	10.2												
NPV 13%	6.4												
NPV 15%	0.0												

funds required to install the completely new plant. To do this we must decide whether the *additional* net cash investment will provide *additional* cash flows sufficient to give a return of more than 10 per cent. The calculations for this are laid out in Table 6.2.

With a negative NPV this means that the incremental investment would not earn an incremental cash flow sufficiently high to meet the criterion rate.

If the two stages had not been separated as shown above and only the replacement proposal been considered, would that have met the criterion rate? Looking at that proposal on its own the values would have been as in Table 6.3.

As can be seen from the table the complete replacement alternative standing on its own would have met the criterion rate and therefore been an acceptable project. However, the incremental investment, the difference between the modernization and the complete replacement alternatives, would not have met that requirement. This means that the extra investment involved would be better spent on another project which does exceed the criterion rate.

Summary

The general approach to multiple-choice problems can be summarized as follows:

1. Evaluate the incremental investment and returns for each alternative.
2. Select the alternative showing the lowest net cash investment and use this as the basis for a normal project evaluation, at this stage ignoring the other alternatives.
3. If this does not meet the criterion rate, abandon that alternative and repeat for the next alternative, i.e. that with the next highest cash investment.
4. When an alternative is found which, on the usual project evaluation, provides a basis for approval, the incremental investment and return between that alternative and the one with the next highest level of investment is appraised.
5. This process is repeated until all alternatives have been appraised.

Leasing versus buying

The availability of leasing facilities provides management with an acceptable method of acquiring the *use* of fixed assets without involving the outlay of cash for their purchase. Whether or not management will use the leasing facility as a means of reducing the capital requirements of the business depends on a number of factors other than the rate of return involved.

Table 6.2

Year	0	1	2	3	4	5	6	7	8	9	10	11	12
	£000s	£000s	£000s	£000s	£000s	£000s	£000s	£000s	£000s	£000s	£000s	£000s	£000s
Cost of new plant	-250.0												
Sale of old plant	5.0												
Cost of modernization	100.00												
Cost saving		22.0	22.0	22.0	22.0	22.0	22.0	22.0	22.0	22.0	22.0		
Tax at 35%			-7.7	-7.7	-7.7	-7.7	-7.7	-7.7	-7.7	-7.7	-7.7	-7.7	
Pool a/c:													
Brought forward	*30.0*												
Added	*250.0*												
Sale proceeds of old plant	*-5.0*												
Cost of modernization taken in Stage 1	*-100.0*												
Capital allowances	*-43.8*	*-32.8*	*-24.6*	*-18.5*	*-13.8*	*-10.4*	*-7.8*	*-5.8*	*-4.4*	*-3.3*	*-2.5*	*-0.4*	
Balance	*131.3*	*98.4*	*73.8*	*55.4*	*41.5*	*31.1*	*23.4*	*17.5*	*13.1*	*9.9*	*7.4*		
Tax saved		15.3	11.5	8.6	6.5	4.8	3.6	2.7	2.0	1.5	1.1	0.9	0.1
Sale of plant												7.0	
Cash flow	-145.0	37.3	25.8	22.9	20.8	19.1	17.9	17.0	16.3	15.8	15.4	0.2	0.1
PV factors 10%	1.000	0.909	0.826	0.751	0.683	0.621	0.564	0.513	0.467	0.424	0.386	0.350	0.319
Present value 10%	-145.0	33.9	21.3	17.2	14.2	11.9	10.1	8.7	7.6	6.7	6.0	0.1	0.0
NPV 10% = -£7,300													

Notes:
1. The investment is the cost of the new plant less the sale proceeds of the existing plant and the outlay that would have been incurred had the modernization proposal been adopted.
2. The 'Pool a/c' has the written-down value of the existing plant brought forward, to which has been added the cost of the new plant. From this has been deducted the sales proceeds of the existing plant and the capital allowances that have been accounted for in Stage 1.

Table 6.3

Year	0 £000s	1 £000s	2 £000s	3 £000s	4 £000s	5 £000s	6 £000s	7 £000s	8 £000s	9 £000s	10 £000s	11 £000s	12 £000s
Investment	−250.0												
Operating cash flow		44.0	44.0	44.0	44.0	44.0	44.0	44.0	44.0	44.0	44.0		
Tax at 35%			−15.4	−15.4	−15.4	−15.4	−15.4	−15.4	−15.4	−15.4	−15.4	−15.4	
Pool a/c:													
Balance brought forward	*30.0*												
Sale of old plant	*−5.0*												
Added	*250.0*												
Capital allowances	*−68.8*	*−51.6*	*−38.7*	*−29.0*	*−21.8*	*−16.3*	*−12.2*	*−9.2*	*−6.9*	*−5.2*	*−3.9*	*−4.6*	
Balance	*206.3*	*154.7*	*116.0*	*87.0*	*65.3*	*48.9*	*36.7*	*27.5*	*20.6*	*15.5*	*11.6*		
Tax saved		24.1	18.0	13.5	10.2	7.6	5.7	4.3	3.2	2.4	1.8	1.4	1.6
Sale of plant												7.0	
Cash flow	−250.0	68.1	46.6	42.1	38.8	36.2	34.5	32.9	31.8	31.0	30.4	−7.0	1.6
PV factors 10%	1.000	0.909	0.826	0.751	0.683	0.621	0.564	0.513	0.467	0.424	0.386	0.350	0.319
Present value 10%	−250.0	61.9	38.5	31.6	26.5	22.5	19.5	16.9	14.9	13.1	11.7	−2.5	0.5

NPV 10% = £5,100

The term 'leasing' in this context is a *finance lease* as defined in Statement of Standard Accounting Practice 21 'Accounting for leases and hire purchase contracts' and is one where the leasing agreement is basically for the working life of the asset and the lease payments amount to over 90 per cent of its fair value. The distinction between leasing and hire-purchase is that a leasing contract does not give the lessee a legal right to acquire the assets, whereas a hire-purchase agreement does give the hirer a legal right to acquire title to the asset on the fulfilment of the contract terms.

While under the terms of SSAP 21 the value of the assets and the payment obligations are disclosed in the balance sheet, the legal ownership of the assets does not lie with the lessee but with the leasing company. This is a factor that may be considered by potential lenders to the business. If a large portion of the assets of the business are held on finance leases then the business has a lower value of 'free' assets against which it might borrow, and a heavier burden of charges against income for lease payments. This means that the ability of the business to borrow money will be reduced.

Shortage of money and an inability to borrow may mean that management has no alternative other than to lease, since this is the only way that the use of the asset can be acquired.

Where management has a choice as to how it acquires the use of assets, the way in which that use is acquired is part of the overall financing strategy of the business. It will weigh up the relative merits of raising finance for the acquisition of assets through purchase, leasing, hire-purchase and any other available methods, and select the mix of methods most applicable to its needs.

When dealing with the choice between leasing and buying, or any other acquisition method, it must be appreciated that the use of non-ownership methods is likely to diminish the ability of the business to fund its capital requirements by borrowing money. One should, therefore, first test whether the commitment of the firm's resources to a project meets the minimum rate of return or other criteria, using the assumption that the assets would be acquired through purchase. If the answer to that is that the project does meet those requirements then the method of acquisition should be appraised as a separate issue.

The outright purchase of assets requires an outlay of money at the beginning of the project. The lease or hire-purchase of assets requires a stream of future rental payments. The question that is posed is: 'Will the outlay of cash for outright acquisition provide a return, in terms of lease payments that will not have to be made, and other differences between the two modes of acquisition, that is sufficient to provide the required rate of return on that investment?' The same incremental principles that have been discussed in this chapter apply equally to this decision.

The cash flow differences between leasing and buying, i.e. those that occur under one alternative but not the other, can be summarized as shown in Table 6.4.

Table 6.4 Cash flow differences—leasing v. buying

Lease	Purchase
—	Capital outlay
Annual lease payments	—
Tax relief on lease payments	—
—	Tax saved by capital allowances
—	Residual values and tax consequences

LEASING AND OPPORTUNITY COSTS

The purchase of an asset that might otherwise have been leased will absorb funds that could have been used for investment in other areas of the business. The use of funds to acquire the asset should only be made where it can earn a higher rate of return based on cash flow differences between leasing and buying than could be earned if those funds were to be used on some other project. In other words we are looking for the opportunity costs of the capital concerned, and the cost of funds will effectively be the return that they could have earned in some other use.

This approach is implicit in other investment decisions, since the allocation of the available resources in any year will involve ranking projects in such a way that none of the projects rejected will have a rate of return that is higher than that of projects approved (after allowing for differences in risk etc.) subject, of course, to the need to conform to the long-term strategy of the business.

This factor is highlighted here so that it is fully appreciated that the lease decision is not dependent on the cost of funds or the criterion rate, except in so far as they define what is an unacceptable rate of return. The critical factor that must be taken into account in making the decision is the return that could be used by deploying the money in other uses.

The leasing decision can be brought into the general capital investment appraisal system by defining the cash outlay that would be involved if the assets are purchased, and comparing this with the increase in the succeeding cash flows that would result from the decision to buy rather than to lease. This then enables the decision to be ranked in the same way as other projects.

Steps in the solution of leasing problems

The logical sequence of steps in making the decision are:

1. Assess the project on the basis that the assets are purchased to see whether it is a project that would qualify for approval under the normal rules.

2. If the project does qualify, then calculate the net cash investment necessary to purchase the assets rather than leasing them.
3. Calculate the incremental cash flows that would arise as between leasing and buying.
4. Calculate the rate of return, or profitability index, represented by the relationship between 2 and 3 above.

Example 6.2
Cracken Woods plc is considering a project that involves replacing its chemical processing installation. The new installation would cost £300,000 and would have an expected life of six years, when new technology might make it obsolescent and it would have no value. The old installation could be sold for £5,000. The new installation should produce cost savings of £112,000 per year.

You have made further enquiries and as a result have received a quotation from a leasing company for the installation. The rental would be £80,000 per year over its economic life of six years, after which it could be leased at a nominal rent.

The company has other projects available that could earn at least 11 per cent after tax.

Stage 1: Evaluation of the project
The first step is to evaluate the project as though the purchase option was to be used. This is set out in Table 6.5, which shows that the project would have a rate of return well in excess of the 11 per cent that is available on other projects and therefore is acceptable.

In this case there is the further opportunity to rent the installation rather than to purchase outright, so the next stage is to see whether the installation should be purchased or leased.

Stage 2
At this stage we are solely concerned with the incremental cash flows between leasing and buying, and must not go back to the cost savings used in Stage 1. The cash flows that we will be concerned with are those outlined earlier:

1. the net saving on rentals;
2. the cash saved by capital allowances;
3. any residual cash flows and tax consequences.

These cash flows and their evaluation are shown in Table 6.6.
The operating cash flows in this case are the rental payments that would not have to be made if the installation is purchased. The capital allowances will be received if the asset is purchased, but not if it is leased. Although

94

Table 6.5 Example 6.2: evaluation of the project on a normal DCF basis

Year	0 £000s	1 £000s	2 £000s	3 £000s	4 £000s	5 £000s	6 £000s	7 £000s	8 £000s
Investment	-300.0								
Sale of old plant	5.0								
Operating cash flow		112.0	112.0	112.0	112.0	112.0	112.0		
Tax 35%			-39.2	-39.2	-39.2	-39.2	-39.2	-39.2	
Pool a/c:									
Added	*300.0*								
Sale of old plant	*-5.0*								
Capital allowances	*-75.0*	*-55.0*	*-41.3*	*-31.0*	*-23.2*	*-17.4*	*-13.1*	*-39.1*	
Balance	*220.0*	*165.0*	*123.8*	*92.8*	*69.6*	*52.2*	*39.1*	*Nil*	
Tax saved		26.3	19.3	14.4	10.9	8.1	6.1	4.6	13.7
Cash flow	-295.0	138.3	92.1	87.2	83.7	80.9	78.9	-34.6	13.7
PV factors 11%	1.000	0.901	0.812	0.731	0.659	0.593	0.535	0.482	0.434
Present value	-295.0	124.6	74.8	63.7	55.2	48.0	42.2	-16.7	5.9

NPV 11% = £102,700

Table 6.6 Example 6.2: evaluation of the lease or buy decision

Year	0 £000s	1 £000s	2 £000s	3 £000s	4 £000s	5 £000s	6 £000s	7 £000s	8 £000s
Investment	−300.0								
Rental saved		80.0	80.0	80.0	80.0	80.0	80.0		
Tax 35%			−28.0	−28.0	−28.0	−28.0	−28.0	−28.0	
Pool a/c:									
Added	*300.0*								
Capital allowances	*−75.0*	*−56.3*	*−42.2*	*−31.6*	*−23.7*	*−17.8*	*−13.3*	*−40.0*	
Balance	*225.0*	*168.8*	*126.6*	*94.9*	*71.2*	*53.4*	*40.0*	*Nil*	
Tax saved		26.3	19.7	14.8	11.1	8.3	6.2	4.7	14.0
Cash flow	−300.0	106.3	71.7	66.8	63.1	60.3	58.2	−23.3	14.0
PV factors 11%	1.000	0.901	0.812	0.731	0.659	0.593	0.535	0.482	0.434
Present value	−300.0	95.8	58.2	48.8	41.6	35.8	31.1	−11.2	6.1
NPV 11% = £6,200									

there is no residual value for the installation the disposal will give further capital allowances. If there had been a residual value this would have been included as it would only be received if the assets are owned.

In this example the cash flow differentials give a rate of return in excess of 11 per cent and therefore the installation should be purchased, unless there are other projects the £300,000 could be used for which would produce a higher rate of return, in which case the assets could still be leased rather than purchased. The profitability index for the project is 306,200/300,000 = 1.02, and it would go into the ranking of projects on that basis.

Note that the sale value of the assets being replaced is not included at this stage since this receipt will occur whether or not the new installation is owned or leased. Therefore it is not a cash flow difference, and is not taken into account. Take the case where an old machine would be sold for £2,000 and a new one purchased for £12,000. The net cash outlay associated with the decision between buying and leasing would be summarized as follows:

	Machine leased £	Machine purchased £
Cash from disposal of old machine	+2,000	+2,000
Purchase price of new machine	—	−12,000
Net cash movement	+2,000	−10,000

The net cash outlay differential between the alternatives of leasing and buying is therefore the difference between −£10,000 and +£2,000, which is the same as the net cost of the new machine. Any cash flow which is common to both of the alternatives under consideration cannot be a cash flow difference and is ignored.

Some lease contracts stipulate that the leasing company undertakes some of the obligations of ownership, such as insurance or maintenance. When one is measuring the rentals for the lease v. buy decision it is the net rental, i.e. after deducting such items, that is relevant.

7. Financing problems

The type of investment problems that have been dealt with so far have been concerned with the allocation of the firm's capital resources to specific uses where profitability has been used to select investments from among a range of options. DCF can, however, also be used when considering the choices open to management in the way in which the business is financed. Management's task is not only to ensure that the rate of return earned by using money in the business is as high as possible, but also to develop a mix of debt and equity in the way in which the business is financed that enhances the return earned for the owners of the business (in the case of companies, the equity shareholders).

Management should examine the relative costs of all the different types of finance that may be used. The first criterion is, of course, that the cost of sources of finance, other than equity, must be *less* than what can be earned when putting those funds to work in the business. For those sources of finance which meet that criterion management needs to identify the mix of funds that provides the optimum return to the equity holders. This optimum mix will be arrived at after considering the level of *gearing* that is appropriate for the business, as will be shown in Chapter 12. Essentially this means the more fixed interest debt that is used to finance the business the higher will be the return to the equity holders. But of course the more debt that is used to finance the business the greater the risk of business failure because of the contractual undertakings required by the lenders. The optimum mix is a trade-off between the higher return and the higher risk.

Within this overall financing strategy laid down by management, the fixed dividend or interest sources need to be examined to see which give the lower present value of overall cost. This requires a comparison of the streams of cash flows associated with servicing each form of finance option. Some problems may also involve outlays of cash in order to *change* from one source of finance to another in order to achieve net cost savings in financing the business.

When the relative streams of cash outlays and cost savings are being considered DCF will have a part to play, but there may also be factors not susceptible to the application of DCF, that may also have to be considered when dealing with specific problems—such as the risks involved.

Sources of funds

One of the purposes in having a number of different sources of capital is to enable the business to appeal to as wide a range of investors as possible by dividing the capital into a number of different classes, each with different income and risk characteristics, that would attract both the speculative and the risk averse investor. The ability to differentiate is limited for non-corporate forms of enterprise to the use of debt or, in the case of partnerships, the limited partners' funds. For companies the scope is much greater, since the shareholders' funds can be divided into any number of classes of share.

Today the decisions made about how the capital is to be raised are more concerned with maximizing the long-term value of the equity holders' funds. To this end the board of directors will create classes of share that best meet the company's requirements. This involves allocating the three following rights in different ways between different classes of share:

1. The right to income
2. The right to repayment
3. The right to vote.

There is no common definition of different classes of share as each company defines its own share capital in its Memorandum and Articles of Association. The classes of share met with in practice are described in general terms below.

PREFERENCE SHARES

Usually this class of share has a prior right to a fixed dividend. That prior right is not against creditors or lenders, but only against other classes of shareholders. Thus the fixed dividend must be paid before any dividend can be paid to, say, ordinary shareholders. This dividend can be either cumulative or non-cumulative. Usually the holders of preference shares will have a prior right to have their capital repaid, again not against creditors, but only against other classes of shareholders. Because of these prior claims there are usually no voting rights.

The dividend is not guaranteed. As with all classes of share, the payment of a dividend is dependent on the company having cumulative realized gains from which the payment can be made, and the directors recommending the payment. Dividends are distributions of earnings and are not tax deductible.

ORDINARY SHARES

This class of share gives rights to all the income that remains after the requirement of all other classes of share have been met, and, when the company is wound up, to all the assets that remain after those prior claims have been met. These are the shareholders who bear the primary risks inherent in business operations, and who hold the voting control. In some cases the ordinary shares may be divided into different groups with different voting rights. This is quite common where two parent companies own the business. It sometimes occurs in listed companies where one class may have votes and another not, although this is frowned upon by the investment community.

99

WED FUNDS

... complete contrast to the funds provided by the various classes of shareholders who actually own the company, money that is borrowed is provided by people who are *creditors* of the business. Since they are not involved in ownership of the company they have no voting rights, and they have an absolute right to receive the interest and loan repayment provided for in the contract. As creditors they may or may not have security against the assets of the company. In the USA 'Other People's Money' (OPM) is often used to describe this source of funds and serves to emphasize the distinction between borrowed money and that provided by the owners. Typical methods of borrowing money are by means of mortgages, debentures and other secured and unsecured loans. The interest paid on borrowed money is a charge against the profits of the business and therefore will be tax deductible.

Factors to take into account in financing decisions

The board of directors, in reaching their decision about how the business is to be financed, should take into account the following factors:

1. The effect the decision will have on the risk of business failure through not being able to meet obligations to creditors.
2. The way the decision may affect the level of gearing and therefore the return to the equity holders.
3. Any possible dilution in the existing shareholders' interest in the capital and income of the business.
4. The effect that the decision may have on the options available in future financing decisions, e.g. if the ability to borrow is fully committed by the present decision it may not be an option in the next financing decision.

THE RISK FACTOR

A decision to add to the funds borrowed by the business will increase the risk element in the financing strategy. Unlike shareholders, people who lend money to the business have a contractual right to the payment of interest and, normally, to the repayment on the due date of the amount lent. It is not in any way related to the ability of the business to pay. The risk to the business is that it may run into a period of poor trading and be unable to meet these commitments and so be put into liquidation. Any additional amount borrowed will increase this possibility and, consequently, increase that risk.

GEARING

The increase in the risk factor for the business also increases the risk attaching to the ordinary shares. Their compensation for this increase in risk is the effect the borrowed money may have on the return earned on their own investment. This matter is more fully covered in Chapter 12.

DILUTION

Listed companies in the United Kingdom are normally obliged to offer new ordinary shares to existing shareholders in proportion to their current holdings, whenever they need to raise new capital by an issue of shares (what are called *pre-emption rights*). This maintains the relative holdings, and therefore voting power, of the individual shareholders.

Sometimes, however, such as when there is a takeover bid or the business enters into association with another company, this does not happen, and consideration must be given to the effect that any issue of shares connected with such transactions may have in diluting the interests of the existing shareholders, particularly if that may affect control of the company.

FLEXIBILITY *from outside*

A decision to borrow £x million for a particular purpose at a particular time cannot be made without considering the effect that it may have on the borrowing powers of the business in the future. There are limits to the capacity of a business to borrow money which are set by the willingness of shareholders to accept the higher risks, and more critically perhaps, the willingness of lenders to lend. The next requirement to raise finance may come at a time when there are economic difficulties which might preclude calling on shareholders to put in more money, and, if the ability to borrow has been used up, then that is no longer an option that can be looked at and the company would be in difficulties.

The ability of a business to borrow money is often looked at in terms of how many times available earnings cover the cost of servicing the interest. The board of directors may therefore at times consider whether it is possible to pay off current borrowing with new borrowing at a lower rate of interest. Since the cost of servicing the debt will be reduced this should provide some room for raising further borrowing at some time in the future.

REFUNDING OPERATIONS

Management should continually monitor the various sources of funds employed to ensure that their cost is kept to a minimum. Differences in the cost of the various sources arise because:

1. Interest rates and preference dividend yields alter, making that source more or less costly compared with the cost of existing funds.
2. Changes take place in the tax structure or rates of tax, at home or overseas, which affect the relative costs of the various sources of capital.
3. New methods of raising finance can evolve which can provide new opportunities for raising capital, e.g. zero rate bonds, perpetual loans.

Interest rates may vary considerably at different stages of the economic cycle. Where a company is borrowing over a 20 to 25 year period, the nominal interest rate may differ markedly from the current market rates during the currency of the loan. Unless there are obstacles to repayment, there are sound arguments for replacing high-cost borrowing in periods of low interest rates. A saving of one per cent after tax is significant when compared with the difficulty of improving the return on capital by a similar amount.

TAXATION

Changes in the tax structure or rates in the tax regime under which the business operates can change the relative cost of different sources of funds. For example, in the UK, where interest on loans has always been a deductible expense for tax purposes, pre-1965 dividends effectively cost a company the net of tax cost; between 1965 and 1973 they then cost the company the gross amount of the dividend, thus effectively increasing their cost relative to the payment of interest. Since 1973 dividends have, in most cases, once again only cost the net of basic rate income tax value and are in fact declared as so many pence per share net of tax. This can be seen in Table 7.1 which illustrates the current UK tax position for a company paying dividends, which uses the present (1989) basic rate of corporation tax.

Table 7.1 The UK tax on companies

	£ millions
Taxable profit	100.0
Corporation tax at 35%	35.0
	65.0
Dividend:	
Net cost	36.0
Retained profit	29.0

The net dividend of £36 million is received in cash by the shareholders. In addition to the net dividend received the shareholders also receive a tax credit to cover their basic tax on the dividend, the rate of which at the present time (1989) is 25 per cent. The net dividend as far as the shareholders are concerned is effectively a gross dividend of £48 million, less the basic income tax rate of 25 per cent, which is £12 million, leaving the net of £36 million. If they do not pay tax then the tax credit can be reclaimed; if they are liable to higher rates of tax, then the difference between the basic rate and the higher rate will have to be paid.

As far as the company is concerned when it pays a dividend it also has to pay to the Inland Revenue something called advance corporation tax (ACT), which is a sum equal to the amount of the tax credits. With an income tax rate of 25 per cent the company would pay ACT to the Inland Revenue of $\frac{25}{75}$ of the cost of any net dividends paid. However, this ACT is not designed to be an extra tax on the company. It can offset the ACT it has paid against its corporation tax payment for the accounting year in which the dividend is actually paid, so that only the balance of the corporation tax (known as 'mainstream' corporation tax) will be payable. However, if the company does not generate sufficient earnings in the UK to cover the gross cost of the dividend then the ACT on the excess will not be recoverable that year. Any under-recovery of ACT can be carried forward by the company. However, if, for example, all the company's earnings come from overseas, then it will be paying no 'mainstream' corporation tax and ACT will in such a case become an extra tax.

The system as presently operated means that companies, other than small companies, will have interest payments relieved at the corporation tax rate of 35 per cent, whereas dividends are effectively relieved at only 25 per cent. Thus a 10 per cent interest rate payable on a loan has an after cost of only 6.5 per cent, whereas a preference share with a dividend rate of 10 per cent would cost the company 10 per cent, since this is a net dividend and both ordinary and preference dividends are subject to the same rules.

Using DCF in refunding operations

Refunding is the term generally used when a business retires one security that it has used in the past to finance its operations, and replaces it with another issue. Often this happens when one issue of long-term debt has to be repaid to the lenders at the end of its life, and it is necessary to replace this source of finance in some way.

This part of the book, however, as suggested earlier, is concerned with a more restricted area of refunding operation: where management is actively considering the retirement of one source of finance, not because its life is drawing to a close, but because it is concerned with the differential between the cost of the existing funds it uses compared with the cost of alternative sources of funds available in the market.

The refunding operation will most probably involve the outlay of some of the firm's cash resources. This would be for expenses connected with the retirement of the old issue and the marketing of the new one, and would include such items as:

1. Any premium payable on the old issue due to its early retirement
2. Expenses of retiring the old issue
3. Expenses of the new issue, e.g. postage, printing, underwriting commission, professional and issuing house fees, etc.
4. Double interest payments if the two issues overlap, or any *additional* costs of bridging finance to cover a period between the redemption of the old issue and the inflow of the funds from the new issue.

This outlay of money will be in competition with the demand for money for other investments within the business in the same way as any other investment project. The investment of £x of the available funds for a refunding operation means that they will not be available for employment elsewhere, and for this reason it must be ascertained whether or not the net savings that can be achieved by this investment represents an adequate return on the cash that is invested, as compared with what can be earned on alternative investments.

SUITABILITY OF DCF AS AN APPRAISAL TOOL FOR THE REFUNDING DECISION

It can be questioned whether DCF is suitable for any stage in the appraisal of a refunding operation. For example, there are other factors which must be taken into account that are of such importance that the decision cannot be taken on rate of return criteria only. It can also be argued that the refunding operation may itself actually enlarge the ability of the company to raise money because of the lower cost for a given amount of finance, and in that sense does not compete with other projects for the funds available.

When the business replaces one loan with another at a lower rate of interest, the burden of debt service on the company is reduced and the interest cover increased. This can create the ability of the business to raise more money and still maintain the pre-refunding interest cover. This is not true if the choice being looked at is the replacement of preference shares with new borrowing. The cost of preference dividends is a distribution of profits and not a charge on profits, and therefore such a proposal would further restrict the borrowing capacity of the business. Both types of refunding can, through the gearing effect on the return on equity, increase the ability to raise new equity finance in the future.

It is submitted, however, that DCF has a role to play in this decision. Irrespective of the effect that the decision may have on the ability of the business to raise additional funds in the future, refunding will absorb some of the capital employed in the business, and if the level of profitability for the business as a whole is to be maintained or improved, such a use of funds should be subject to the same tests as any other use. Certainly the rate of return criterion will not necessarily be the deciding factor, but the rate of return that can be earned by using funds in this way should be taken into account when the decision is made.

Before examining the way in which the data should be handled in making the appraisal, it should be pointed out that there is relatively little risk attached to this type of decision. The future savings can be accurately measured as they are the difference between the contractual rate of interest or dividend, and the cost factors in the net cash investment which should be capable of close estimation.

NET CASH INVESTMENT

The net cash investment in a refunding operation consists of the various expenses noted on page 103. In addition to the outlays themselves, their tax consequences must be considered. In general the incidental expenses connected with obtaining loan finance which carries deductible interest are allowed for tax purposes. This would include such items as costs relating to the repayment of and providing security for the loan. It would not include stamp duty, foreign exchange losses, repayment premiums or issue discounts. These provisions also apply to convertible loan stocks (i.e. those where the holder has the right to convert the loan into ordinary shares at some future date). Any additional interest costs incurred during the change-over period will be allowable for tax purposes as revenue expenses.

ANNUAL COST SAVINGS

The return from the net cash investment is the savings in cost between the interest of fixed dividend payable on the old issue, and that payable on the new issue. As far as the interest element in such calculations is concerned it is the after-tax cost that is the relevant value. Fixed dividends on preference shares are already the after-tax value.

TIME HORIZON

Normally the length of time an existing issue has still to run will be less than the life of the new issue that replaces it. If, for example, it is proposed to replace a loan that has another ten years to run, it will probably be by a loan with a longer life, e.g. twenty to twenty-five years. At the time the decision is made one cannot tell what the financing choices will be after the ten year period of the existing loan ends. This would therefore inhibit any comparison beyond the life of the existing loan, and since residual values are not appropriate to this type of decision the life of the project would be ten years.

Example 7.1

Peraco plc has outstanding an issue of £15 million of 12 per cent unsecured loan stock that has a further twelve years to run before it must be repaid. The company has the option of repaying the loan at any time before maturity at a premium of 3 per cent. Since the issue was made, interest rates have fallen, and the company is now considering replacing that issue with an issue of £15m of 9 per cent debentures with a life of 25 years.

It is expected that the costs of the new issue would be £350,000, of which £200,000 would be allowable for tax. The new issue would be made two months before the repayment of the old issue and the company expects to be able to earn 8 per cent on the short-term placing of the surplus cash.

The tax rate is 35 per cent and the company has other projects available that would earn 10 per cent after tax. If implemented the replacement would take place at the beginning of the company's accounting year so that the costs and first year's savings would occur in the same accounting period.

The problem should be tackled by looking at the two major elements of net cash investment and annual cash flows. As the annual savings are a constant value over the life of the project the present value of these can be arrived at by using the tables for the present value of £1 receivable *each* year as shown in Appendix B. The relevant computations are shown in Table 7.2.

Table 7.2 Example 7.1: evaluating the exchange of one form of borrowing for another

	£000s
1. *Net cash investment*:	
Expenses of new issue	−350.0
Premium of redemption of old issue	−450.0
Net interest cost for two months	−25.0
Tax relief on £200,000 plus £25,000 − 225 × 35% × 0.909	71.6
Present value	−753.4
2. *Annual cash flows:*	
Annual interest saving 12% − 9% on £15m = £450,000 per year:	
Year 0	450.0
Years 1 to 11: 450.0 × 6.495 =	2,922.7
Tax on savings:	
£450,000 p.a. × 0.35 = 157.5 p.a.	
Years 1 to 12: 157.5 × 6.814 =	−1,073.2
Present value	1,299.5

From the figures in Table 7.2 it can be seen that the present value of the savings is greater than the investment, therefore the project earns a higher rate of return than alternative projects. Discounted at the 10 per cent rate the project has a profitability index of 1,299.5/753.4 = 1.72.

Example 7.2
The board of directors of Stampo plc have recently considered the position of the preference shares issued by their company. The nominal value of the shares amounts to £1 million and carries a cumulative dividend of 7 per cent. It would be possible to persuade the preference shareholders to have their shares redeemed by offering 110p for each £1 share which would include any accrued dividend. The directors estimate that they could issue an unsecured loan of £1 million repayable in 20 years time, carrying an interest rate of 8 per cent.

The directors propose to redeem the preference shares on 1 March and to make the unsecured loan issue on 1 May. Bridging finance would be available at 10 per cent. In addition there would be expenses of £30,000, half of which would be allowable for tax. The board has laid down that any project must earn at least 12 per cent after tax. The current tax rate is 35 per cent. The decision is being made in the second half of the company's financial year and, since the interest on the new loan will be paid half-yearly in arrears, the first year's savings would occur in the year following the refunding operation.

Table 7.3 Evaluation of replacement of preference shares by borrowing

	£000s	£000s
1. *Net cash investment*		
Premium on redemption of preference shares		−100.0
Expenses of redemption and new issue		−30.0
Interest on bridging finance: $£1m \times 0.10 \times \frac{2}{12}$	−16.7	
Tax relief on interest:		
$16.7 \times 0.35 \times \frac{2}{12} = 9.7 \times 0.893$	8.7	
		−8.0
Tax relief on $\frac{1}{2}$ expenses: $15.0 \times 0.35 \times 0.893$		4.7
Total net cash investment		−133.3
2. *Annual cash flows*		
Annual saving (net):		
Cost of 7% dividend: 70.0×7.469		522.8
Cost of 8 per cent interest:		
-80.0 years 1 to 20 $= -80.0 \times 7.469$	−597.5	
Tax relief on interest:		
$80.0 \times 0.35 = 28.0 \times 6.669$[1]	186.7	
		−410.8
		112.0

1. This is the present value factor for 12 per cent for years 2 to 21 and is found by taking the factor for years 1 to 21 and deducting the factor for the year that is not required, in this case year 1.

The computations for this evaluation are given in Table 7.3. In this case the present value of the savings is less than the investment when discounted at the criterion rate so the project is not acceptable. Note that, although the interest rate is higher than the preference dividend rate, since the former is relievable for tax it produces a cost saving in the relevant years.

There is one further factor which perhaps should be considered in the above example. If the preference issue is not redeemed then ACT will be payable each time the dividend is paid. This will be relieved against the mainstream corporation tax payable in the following year, but this timing difference may be significant. On the £70,000 dividend each year ACT will be $\frac{25}{75}$ at 1989 rates, which is £23,333. The present value of that stream of payments is £23,333 × 7.469 = £174,274. The present value of the relief for ACT one year later is £23,333 × 6.669 = £155,607. This is a difference of £18,667, which represents a further saving if the company proceeds with the refunding. This would make the present value of the savings £130,600 and result in the project nearly meeting the criterion rate.

Evaluating alternative issues

When additional finance is to be raised management's task is to select the sources of finance which will provide the best return to the shareholders. The board of directors must therefore first look at the question of whether to finance through an issue of ordinary shares or by way of borrowing more money, or through issuing preference shares. If the choice is to raise money at fixed dividend or interest rates, then it wants to do so in a way that has the least total present value of cost.

Different ways of raising capital at fixed rates of dividend or interest will have different patterns of cash flow, the streams of payments being made up of interest or fixed dividend, and in the case of borrowed money, the repayment of principal. DCF can be used to select the proposed alternative which has the lowest present value and which will, as a consequence, enhance the future value of the shareholders' funds. This is perhaps best understood if it is appreciated that the discounted value of the shareholders' funds is the future profit potential of the business, less the future stream of payments for the finance necessary to support that future profit potential. The lower the present value of the financing outgoings, the greater the present value left for the owners of the business.

Used in this way DCF is not comparing a cash outlay with inward cash flows. The problem is solely concerned with the present value of future streams of payments. The differences that are being compared are the timing of the future payments, differences in the cost of interest, etc., and the pattern of repayments of the principal sum.

Example 7.3
Copond plc is going through a period of rapid expansion, and the board of directors are considering raising extra funds to finance that growth. It has been decided that the new money will be raised by borrowing rather than a rights issue to ordinary shareholders. An extra £4 million is required to carry the business over the next few years, and the board have been presented with two proposals for borrowing that amount.

Proposal A is to raise an unsecured loan of £4 million carrying an interest rate of $10\frac{1}{4}$ per cent with the whole of the principal repayable at the end of 25 years.

Proposal B is to issue £4 million 10 per cent debentures with a life of 25 years. No repayments of principal would be made for the first five years, but thereafter £200,000 of the debentures must be redeemed at the end of each year.

The current rate of tax is 35 per cent and the company can earn 10 per cent on the funds employed in the business.

To make a decision on which source of finance to use one should calculate the net cash outgoings in respect of each alternative. Using the criterion rate of return these cash flows are then discounted back to their present value, and the total present value of each compared. This process is shown in Tables 7.4 and 7.5, from which it can be seen that the net present value of the stream of payments that would result from the selection of Proposal A is less than that for Proposal B, and therefore Proposal A would be more advantageous for the business.

Table 7.4 Example 7.3: present value of payments for unsecured loan

	£000s
Annual interest cost : £4m × 0.1025 × 9.077	3,721.6
Tax relief: £4m × 0.1025 × 0.35 × 8.251	−1,184.0
Repayment of principal, year 25: £4m × 0.092	368.0
	2,905.6

The sum of the actual payments in respect of A are higher than the actual payments in respect of B, since the whole of the principal is outstanding for the whole of the period. If the rate of discounting being used is directly related to the return that can be earned by the employment of funds within the business, this 'stretching' of the repayments right up to the end of the loan period more than compensates for the extra costs involved.

In common with other financing problems there will be a number of other factors to take into account. In this example the two principal ones that would need to be considered are:

1. The debenture proposal would involve giving the lender(s) a charge over some or all of the assets of the business, and this might reduce the ability of the business to raise additional borrowed funds in the future.
2. Proposal B provides for earlier payment of the principal sum, therefore the debt/equity ratio of the company will fall steadily after the fifth year, quite apart from any change due to increases in shareholders' funds. This provides extra debt capacity in later years when the ratio has been substantially reduced.

Table 7.5 Example 7.3: present value of payments for debenture issue

Year	Interest after tax £000s	Repayment of principal £000s	Total payments £000s	PV factor for 10%	Present value £000s
1	260.0		260.0	0.909	236.3
2	260.0		260.0	0.826	214.8
3	260.0		260.0	0.751	195.3
4	260.0		260.0	0.683	177.6
5	260.0		260.0	0.621	161.5
6	260.0	200.0	460.0	0.564	259.4
7	247.0	200.0	447.0	0.513	229.3
8	234.0	200.0	434.0	0.467	202.7
9	221.0	200.0	421.0	0.424	178.5
10	208.0	200.0	408.0	0.386	157.5
11	195.0	200.0	395.0	0.350	138.2
12	182.0	200.0	382.0	0.319	121.9
13	169.0	200.0	369.0	0.290	107.0
14	156.0	200.0	356.0	0.263	93.6
15	143.0	200.0	343.0	0.239	82.0
16	130.0	200.0	330.0	0.218	71.9
17	117.0	200.0	317.0	0.198	62.8
18	104.0	200.0	304.0	0.180	54.7
19	91.0	200.0	291.0	0.164	47.7
20	78.0	200.0	278.0	0.149	41.4
21	65.0	200.0	265.0	0.135	35.8
22	52.0	200.0	252.0	0.123	31.0
23	39.0	200.0	239.0	0.112	26.8
24	26.0	200.0	226.0	0.102	23.1
25	13.0	200.0	213.0	0.092	19.6

Total present value of cash flows   2,970.4

DCF and investment in shares

One area where there has been little application of DCF is in the field of in-vestment in the shares of listed companies. This contrasts with the use of the technique in bond yield tables which show the return to maturity of investing in fixed interest stocks, principally, of course, government bonds. The use of DCF in share investments is dealt with here because it may have some rele-vance to the methods of determining the cost of capital dealt with in Chapter 12. The attitude of investors is of importance in that context, particularly the way in which they regard the return appropriate to individual shares.

An investment in shares is usually made with two objectives: to provide an annual return in the form of dividends, and to secure a capital apprecia-tion in the value of the shares when sold. These are the two elements which make up the overall return on an investment. When comparing alternative investments, both of these factors are considered, together with the risks inherent in each, and the investment showing the highest combined return will be selected allowing for any risk differential. The pattern of cash flows for an investment in shares is similar to that for an investment in plant and machinery. There is an initial outlay of cash for the purchase of the shares and related costs, followed by a series of annual cash flows from net dividends, and a residual value made up of the sale value of the shares less related costs. The residual values here will, of course, be more significant than those for plant and machinery.

The net dividend will be adjusted for the tax status of the investor. If it is a tax exempt fund, the tax credit will be reclaimed adding to the net dividend. If the individual pays the higher rate of tax, this will further reduce the net dividend. The tax position on capital gains will also have to be considered. Companies, for example, will be taxed at the corporation tax rate on any gain; individuals will pay tax at their marginal income tax rate on any gain, but they have the advantage of a nil tax rate band. Tax exempt entities do not pay any capital gains tax.

Example 7.4
Mr AB is considering the purchase of 2,000 ordinary shares in Anonymous plc. The current price to buy the shares is 250p each and the expenses of the purchase would be £142. The shares are to be purchased as an investment and Mr AB's evaluation of them is based upon an assumption that the current net dividend of 11.75p per share will increase to 13.2p in the third year after purchase and to 14.7p in the fourth year. He would expect to sell the holding at the end of the fourth year at a price of 350p each, incurring selling costs of £130. He assumes that sundry other investments would have used up his capital gains tax zero rate band, and his marginal rate of tax is 25 per cent but the gain will take it up to 40 per cent. He estimates that indexation will add 20 per cent to the cost of the shares by the time that he sells them.

The method of calculating the rate of return on this investment is shown in Tables 7.6 and 7.7. The use of DCF in appraising the relative merits of alternative investments requires a great deal of discipline in evaluating the variables that must be taken into account. It is no longer a situation where one says 'I will buy this share as I expect the dividend will rise and there will be

Table 7.6 Example 7.4: net cash investment

	£
Purchase price of shares	5,000
Purchase costs	142
Total cost	5,142

Table 7.7 Example 7.4: annual and residual cash flows

Year	Net dividends £	PV factors for 11%	Present value £	PV factors for 10%	Present value £
1	235.0	0.901	211.7	0.909	213.6
2	235.0	0.812	190.8	0.826	194.1
3	264.0	0.731	193.0	0.751	198.3
4	294.0	0.659	193.7	0.683	200.8

Residual value[1]

	6,590.0	0.659	4,342.8	0.683	4,501.0
	7,618.0		5,132.0		5,307.8

		£
1.	Residual value calculated as follows:	
	Sale value of shares	7,000
	Less Expenses of sale	130
		6,870
	Capital gains tax: cost 5,142 indexed to 6,170:	
	Net sale proceeds 6,870 − 6,170 × 40% =	280
		6,590

a rise in the price of the shares.' Explicit values must be placed on all of the factors involved.

It can be seen from the table that if Mr AB's expectations are fulfilled then the rate of return over the four year investment would be almost 11 per cent.

Turning to the cost of capital to a business, it will be seen that the cost of the ordinary shareholders' funds will be based largely on the long-term return that investors expect from purchasing the company's shares. This will be compared with that which could be earned from investments in the shares of other companies and other forms of investment, and there will be some movement towards a common yardstick of return.

8. *The uncertainty of the future*

So far in this book it has been assumed that it is possible to establish a single outcome for a particular project, and the judgement as to whether or not to go ahead with the project has been based upon that 'most likely' value. In real life, of course, one cannot be certain that that one predicted outcome will actually occur. For a variety of reasons the actual outcome may be better or worse than that which was used as the basis for the decision. It is this almost certain variability of future returns that poses risks to a business.

The management of a business will always be faced with making decisions about the future of that business. The problem is that the future by its very nature cannot be certain. While one might have a view of the outcome of some future event, the actual outcome may turn out to be quite different for a number of reasons—technology may change, new competitors emerge, governments may change policies, consumer preferences change, and so on. In the decision-making process, factors that are the closest in time are likely to be more certain, whereas those that are the furthest away in time are likely to be much more uncertain because of the longer time horizon. So while management should quite properly take steps to minimize the level of risk, it is something that cannot be avoided altogether.

Decisions relating to capital investment are among the most difficult, and at the same time the most critical, that management will have to make. Difficult, because, with the usually long time horizons involved, the data on which they will be based will be increasingly uncertain as one goes further into the future. To deal with these uncertainties it is necessary, in some way, to put values on the range of possible outcomes of projects, which is not an easy process. These difficulties are enhanced by the increasing rapidity of change. In a modern industrial society, and one in which sophisticated financial and other services are deployed, the rate of change has increased enormously in recent years and shows no sign of abating. Indeed, the forecasting of the future environment within which the business will operate is a hazardous process fraught with problems, nevertheless it is one that has to be dealt with.

These problems are compounded by changes in the fiscal and economic environment within which a business operates. In particular inflation may have an important impact on the outcome of a project. Management should have a strategy for ensuring that the business takes account of inflation in its pricing policies etc., but there may be contractual or political factors which might inhibit that. The biggest problem that it poses is, however, how does one forecast what the rate of inflation will be in two or three years time, let alone in fifteen or twenty years.

The decisions being taken are also critical in that they will have far reaching consequences for the profitability of the business for many years into the future; they usually deal with substantial amounts of the capital of the business, and once that capital is committed to specific uses, it is likely to be difficult to release it for other projects if things go wrong. Individual decisions may in some cases be substantial enough to affect the underlying structure of the business and its entire operational base.

Management's attitude to risk

Management must itself develop a policy relating to the tolerable degree of risk. Is it to be risk tolerant, prepared to assume a high-risk profile in order to gain higher than normal profit growth and be prepared to live with the consequences of such a policy? Or will it be risk averse, trying to minimize risks at all costs, as far as is possible? Even though that may result in lower profit growth management may have fewer sleepless nights. Indeed, is it the prerogative of management to make such a decision? After all, as far as companies are concerned, the business is owned by the shareholders who should perhaps be the people who should make such a decision. Unless they are the same group of people as the management (which may be the case where the company is privately owned), they may have divergent views.

While in practice it is likely that the management of the publicly held company will determine its attitude to risk, it has to be born in mind that shareholders may sit in judgement on them if the outcome of their decision results in low profit growth. Management might be removed, for example, as the result of a takeover bid, or the shareholders may vote with their feet by selling their stake in the company, thus substantially lowering its market value. Many senior managers believe that investors take too much of a short-term view of companies when making their investment decisions, but it is a fact of life that they have to come to terms with.

Determinants of risk

Risk will arise because, when setting the framework of operations in the long-term planning process (dealt with in Chapter 12), management is making a series of judgements about what the future holds for the business and how it will cope with changing circumstances. Some of the key decisions about the future relate to such matters as:

1. Selecting the right mix of products or services
2. The way in which those goods or services are marketed
3. The way in which they are produced
4. The way in which the business as a whole is financed.

114

MIX OF GOODS OR SERVICES

The selection of the future mix of goods or services is part of the process of developing the corporate strategy. Strategic planning can be used to minimize the risks that are undertaken in developing a particular product mix. If the mix of products selected is one where a large proportion of those products or services have high-risk profiles, then the business as a whole is likely to become one with a higher risk characteristic. If it is felt desirable to avoid such a trend, then one should be looking for some balance in the risk profiles, combining some key products with high risk/return characteristics with some where the outcome is more certain.

MARKETING RISKS

The way in which products and services are marketed can also affect the risk factor. There are different strategies for launching a new product. A high-risk strategy could be adopted to try, early in the life cycle of the product, to capture a major part of the market and to some extent pre-empt the competition, but which could be very costly should it fail. Or a more cautious policy could be adopted which might produce a lower market share but have a much lower effect on overall profit if it proves to be wrong.

PRODUCTION RISKS

Here again there are high-risk and low-risk strategies which might be adopted. Sophisticated, costly equipment, which is highly cost effective, might be specific to that product and have no other use should the market for that product fail. If the product is a success then the business will reap the benefits of the low costs that would ensue; if it fails then the equipment may become a costly white elephant.

FINANCING RISKS

The balance of the reward and risk elements in the way in which the business is financed is one which is dealt with elsewhere in this book. In general it is likely to be the case that the higher the level of debt that is used to finance the business the lower will be the cost of capital and the higher the gearing effect on the return to shareholders. However, at the same time the more the business relies on debt finance, the higher the risk of business failure because of its fixed commitments to pay interest, etc. Even more critical is too great a reliance on short-term credit. This can be withdrawn at any time leaving the business in a position where it cannot meet its commitments to creditors. This is perhaps the greatest reason why so many new small businesses fail.

Dangers in avoiding risk

While it is quite proper for management to try to minimize risk, it must not avoid taking on high-risk projects at all costs. It might be thought that a policy of only accepting projects with the minimum of risk, i.e. by deciding not to proceed with projects that contain significant elements of risk, management can shield the business from the consequences of risk. Further thought will show that this is not necessarily the case. Typically, the riskiest investment proposals are those concerned with research and development expenditure and launching new products or services. These expenditures, however, are essential if a business is to survive and grow. They are the seed corn for the future. Any business that does not generate new ideas and products is likely to be overtaken by those businesses that are prepared to spend money in that way. The task of management should be to try to ensure that as high a proportion of high-risk projects as is possible are successful, so that the advantages of those successes outweigh the costs of the failures.

If the management of a business feels unable to accept the uncertainties inherent in such investment proposals, or becomes unwilling to take on the risks associated with making such decisions, that business is likely to become stagnant. In other words, failure to invest in the riskier projects that will take the business forward into the future exposes the business to a much greater risk—that of being overtaken in the market place and left behind by competitors with innovative products and ideas, with the long-term consequences that such a situation would have.

Quality of data

If management is to make decisions about projects whose future returns are highly variable, that is to say include a high degree of risk, then it should have available, when making those decisions, data that sets out how variable those returns are likely to be and the probability of the possible outcomes. For example, if one was assessing the two projects shown in Figure 8.1, then project A has little probability of major variations from the expected rate of return, whereas project B shows a high probability of major variation from the expected rate of return.

How the probability of variations happening can be assessed is explored in the next chapter, but it does mean that more information about projects will have to be produced and the decision-making process expanded to take into account judgemental factors, such as probability. So far, for example, we have started assessing a project assuming that all the planning has taken place to produce the probable values for the operating cash flow. This planning will have been based upon the conventional planning/budgeting process. We have then looked at other factors that affect cash flow, such as taxation, in order to arrive at the year-by-year cash flows.

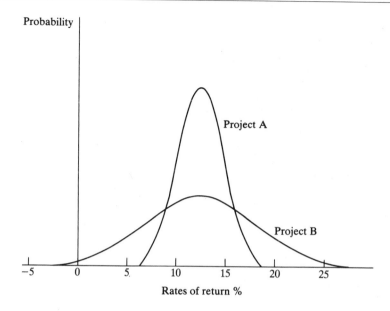

Figure 8.1 Variability of rates of return

If management is to acquire an in-depth perception of a project it will be necessary to go back to the original planning data, e.g. sales, selling price, labour costs, etc., and calculate the rate of return directly from this basic data. It is then necessary to assess the variability of these various elements that make up the project. It might then be possible to provide management with a better information bank on which to base its decision, through two different routes:

1. Through some form of *probability* assessment to produce a probability distribution of the rate of return on a project, such as those shown for the two projects in Figure 8.1.
2. Through some form of *sensitivity* analysis to establish how the rate of return would vary given variations in the underlying operating elements of the project, such as changes in labour costs or prices of products.

Minimizing risk

Given that management has made its decision about its attitude to risk, then within the level of risk that it has decided upon, consideration should be given to how major high-risk projects can be undertaken while at the same time keeping the risks to the business as a whole at a minimum. Risk management has been developed in a number of business areas such as exposure to foreign exchange risks. The same basic principles should be adapted in planning its investment strategy.

117

DIVERSIFICATION

This has been a conventional method of minimizing risk for many years. The basic idea is that if the business has a sufficient spread of activities, if things go wrong in one area they may be compensated for by better than normal performance in another. Many businesses have relied on this philosophy over the years and it has seemed to serve them well. Today, however, it is being questioned for a number of reasons, perhaps the most persuasive of which is that the very diversity of activities makes it difficult for top management to control everything that is happening, that there is a limit to the extent to which one can stretch management skills.

More recently the trend has been to concentrate on 'core' activities and divest the business of peripheral activities. Even here, however, management usually identifies a number of core activities so that the business as a whole has a sufficient spread of different activities to provide enough diversity to give the business some protection should there be difficulties in one of the core activities.

PORTFOLIO OF ACTIVITIES

It follows from what has been said so far that any investment appraisal system cannot rely solely on the financial assessment by rate of return. The strategic planning process should identify a spread of activities which meets the perceived risk profile of the business that management has set, while at the same time limiting overall risk as far as possible. It must also take into account other long-term requirements for a successful business. This spread of activities should be designed:

1. To produce a balance of projects between those with a bias towards early cash flows and those with a bias towards later cash flows so that the overall cash flow pattern does not have major deviations from year to year.
2. To ensure that they provide for an even increment in profits over the years, rather than a pattern where there are periods of sharply declining profits as new projects are brought on stream.
3. To maintain a planned balance between high-risk and minimum-risk projects.
4. To minimize any adverse effects of changes in the national or industry economic situation through investing in areas which are counter-cyclical, that is to invest in areas that will do well at different stages in the business cycle.

Only when the above matters have been resolved should one begin to look at the technical ways by which management can get a better insight into the projects that are submitted to them for approval.

9. *Dealing with risk in investment decisions*

Role of DCF in handling risk and uncertainty

When appraising a project where there is an element of risk, management will be assisted in the decision-making process if it has some idea of the magnitude of uncertainty, for the extent of uncertainty determines the degree of risk inherent in the project. If there was no uncertainty then there would be no risk, other than that resulting from bad decisions.

Given that there will always be some uncertainty in investment decisions, the appraisal process should take that into account. DCF is more rigorous in the analysis of information for making investment decisions than other appraisal methods, and it should be adapted to provide some indication of the degree of uncertainty in the various projects. This adaptation should be extended so that DCF can establish the possible outcomes of a particular project, together with an assessment of the probabilities of those outcomes.

When projects are submitted to management for approval the typical response of those concerned with the approval process is to ask 'What if . . .' questions. For example, 'What will the rate of return be if sales are 10 per cent less than those forecast?' 'What if labour costs are higher than those allowed for?' If the appraisal system can enable answers to be given to these questions, together with an indication as to how sensitive the rate of return is to changes in the various factors that may be called into question in such a way, then management has a much more rational basis for making its investment decisions.

USE OF THE COMPUTER

A sophisticated system for analysing risk and uncertainty, and to measure the effects of changes in any of the component factors, will usually require the use of a computer. This book will not attempt to go into the detailed aspects of programming that would be involved, but instead will outline approaches that can be followed by programmers and others. There are standard packages available for the purpose, but management may require procedures which reflect their particular needs and which must be dealt with on an individual basis.

With modern small computers and spreadsheet programs it is possible for managers and others to build a model of the project that is the subject of appraisal. The different variables can be identified together with the inter-relationship between all aspects of a project. These can then be replicated on

119

a spreadsheet in a way that enables a range of values to be looked at for the different elements of the project, and the implication that those changes have for the rate of return.

Estimating the range of rates of return without a computer

When, for any reason, it is impossible, or impracticable, to use a computer for this type of problem, a manual method that will show an approximation of the spread of possible rates of return can be developed. So far in this book, assumptions have been made that there is only a single value for all of the elements of the project, e.g. 'The project has a life of ten years', 'The rate of tax is 35 per cent', and so on. In real life this is not the case. While there may be a 'most likely' value, there is also the possibility that other values will arise as the project proceeds because of the inherent uncertainties, and some assessment of the other possible values is required.

ESTABLISHING THE RANGE OF VALUES

The first step in risk analysis is to start asking about the possible limits in both directions for all the values that are to be used in appraising the project. If the increase in operating cash flows is estimated to be £50,000 per year, one should explore how much higher or lower that cash flow could be, and it may be that it is estimated with a degree of certainty that it should not exceed £60,000, nor be lower than, say, £40,000, with the £50,000 being the most likely value that will be achieved.

This process can be repeated for all the factors that are to be used in the appraisal, so that for each of them we have values for the possible upper and lower limits, as well as the most expected values. This provides us, for all or some of the elements of the project, three values:

1. The 'possible best' value
2. The 'most probable' value
3. The 'possible worst' value.

Using all the 'possible best' values for the elements of the project we can then calculate the 'possible best' rate of return; by taking all of the 'most probable' values we can calculate the 'most probable' rate of return; and taking all of the 'possible worst' values we can calculate the 'possible worst' rate of return. This would give management some indication of the limits within which the rate of return should fall. However, it does not give any indication of the *probability* of any particular rate of return.

Example 9.1
An investment project involves an estimated outlay of £200,000, and the limits to that outlay are believed to be £190,000 and £220,000. The increase

in operating cash flows is expected to be between £52,000 and £60,000, with the most likely value being £55,000. Depending on the impact of technological change, the project should have a useful life of between four and seven years, the most likely period being five years. At the end of the fourth year the residual value of the plant is expected to be £12,000, after the fifth year £4,000, and after the seventh year £1,000. No change can be foreseen in the rate of taxation which is currently 35 per cent, or in the rate of capital allowances.

What is the most likely rate of return on the project, and the upper and lower rates of return that might be achieved?

The calculations in Table 9.1 indicate that if the project achieves the most likely values the rate of return would be about 9 per cent. If we now look at the possible worst values that might emerge for the project the figures would look like those shown in Table 9.2.

From Table 9.2 it can be seen that the net cash flows over the life of the project are nil, i.e. the total of the positive values equals that of the negative values. This means that the rate of return that would be achieved if the project met all of the worst predictions would be zero.

Looking at the most favourable outcomes for the project the values would look like those in Table 9.3. From the table it can be seen that the best possible outcome for the project would produce a rate of return of just over 20 per cent.

While the above calculations show the range of outcomes that might arise if the project is given the go-ahead, it has not provided any indication of the *probability* of any particular rate of return being achieved.

DISTRIBUTION CURVE OF RATES OF RETURN

The 'best' and 'worst' outcomes will have a much lower probability of occurring than the 'most likely' rate of return. From the nature of probability theory it is possible to give some indication of the probability of the various possible outcomes of the project. The shape of a probability distribution curve is something like that shown in Figure 9.1, which relates to Example 9.1 above. Point A on the distribution curve is the possible 'worst' outcome; Point C is the possible 'best' outcome and Point B the 'most likely' outcome. The approximate probability of any other rate of return being achieved can then be read off from the graph.

Assessing probability using the computer

The upper and lower rates of return calculated for Example 9.1 were based on the assumption that *all* the most favourable predictions or *all* the least favourable predictions will happen together. As a result Figure 9.1 gives

Table 9.1 Example 9.1: calculation of the most probable rate of return

Year	0 £000s	1 £000s	2 £000s	3 £000s	4 £000s	5 £000s	6 £000s	7 £000s
Investment	−200.0							
Operating cash flow		55.0	55.0	55.0	55.0	55.0		
Tax @ 35%			−19.2	−19.2	−19.3	−19.2	−19.3	
Pool a/c:								
Added	*200.0*							
	−50.0							
Capital allowances	*150.0*	*−37.5*	*−28.1*	*−21.1*	*−15.8*	*−11.9*	*−31.6*	
Pool balance		*112.5*	*84.4*	*63.3*	*47.5*	*35.6*	*Nil*	
Tax saved		17.5	13.1	9.8	7.4	5.5	4.2	11.1
Sale of plant							4.0	
Cash flow	−200.0	72.5	48.9	45.6	43.1	41.3	−11.1	11.1
PV factors for 9%	1.000	0.917	0.842	0.772	0.708	0.650	0.596	0.547
Present value	−200.0	66.5	41.2	35.2	30.5	26.8	−6.6	6.0
Total PV: −0.4								

Table 9.2 Example 9.1: calculation of the possible worst rate of return

Year	0 £000s	1 £000s	2 £000s	3 £000s	4 £000s	5 £000s	6 £000s
Investment	-220.0						
Operating cash flow		52.0	52.0	52.0	52.0		
Tax @ 35%			-18.2	-18.2	-18.2	-18.2	
Pool a/c:							
Added	*220.0*						
Capital allowances	*-55.0*	*-41.3*	*-30.9*	*-23.2*	*-17.4*	*-40.2*	
Pool balance	*165.0*	*123.8*	*92.8*	*69.6*	*52.2*	*Nil*	
Tax saved		19.3	14.4	10.8	8.1	6.1	14.1
Sale of plant						12.0	
Cash flow	-220.0	71.3	48.2	44.6	41.9	-0.1	14.1
Net total cash flow £0.0							

Table 9.3 Example 9.1: calculation of the best possible rate of return

Year	0 £000s	1 £000s	2 £000s	3 £000s	4 £000s	5 £000s	6 £000s	7 £000s	8 £000s	9 £000s
Investment	-190.00									
Operating cash flows		60.0	60.0	60.0	60.0	60.0	60.0	60.0		
Tax @ 35%			-21.0	-21.0	-21.0	-21.0	-21.0	-21.0	-21.0	
Pool a/c:										
Added	*190.0*									
Capital allowances	*-47.5*	*-35.6*	*-26.7*	*-20.0*	*-15.0*	*-11.3*	*-8.5*	*-6.3*	*-18.0*	
Pool balance	*142.5*	*106.9*	*80.2*	*60.1*	*45.1*	*33.8*	*25.4*	*19.0*	*Nil*	
Tax saved		16.6	12.5	9.4	7.0	5.3	3.9	3.0	2.2	6.3
Sale of plant									1.0	
Cash flow	-190.0	76.6	51.5	48.4	46.0	44.3	42.9	42.0	-17.8	6.3
PV factors 20%	1.000	0.833	0.694	0.579	0.482	0.402	0.335	0.279	0.233	0.194
Present value	-190.0	63.8	35.7	28.0	22.2	17.8	14.4	11.7	-4.1	1.2
NPV +0.7										

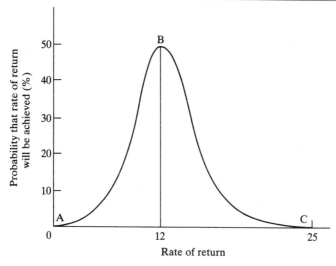

Figure 9.1 Example 9.1: Approximate distribution curve of rates of return

only some indication of the degree of probability of achieving intermediate rates of return. A more subtle tool is needed if management is to be able to forecast the real distribution curve of possible rates of return for a project.

In real life it is likely that in the final result there will be a combination of good and bad outcomes for the various elements in a project. The way in which such outcomes combine in any particular circumstance will depend upon the degree of probability of the various values for each of the elements that make up the project as a whole. This probability will in turn depend upon the distribution curve of probabilities for that element.

If one produces a probability distribution of the values for each element in the project, then the rate of return that results from a random combination of the values for each element—taking into account the probability of any value occurring—is a reflection of those values and their probability. The advent of the computer enables one to carry out a series of calculations of the rate of return using such data. Each computation picks a random value for each element based upon its probability distribution. The rate of return resulting from each calculation is plotted on a graph and gradually builds up a probability distribution curve for the project as a whole such as that shown in Figure 9.2.

Probability analysis of elements of the project

To enable the above analytical technique to be used, once the basic elements of the project have been identified it is then necessary to draw up some probability distribution for the range of values that may occur for that element. Managers may be reluctant to estimate such data because of the uncertain-

125

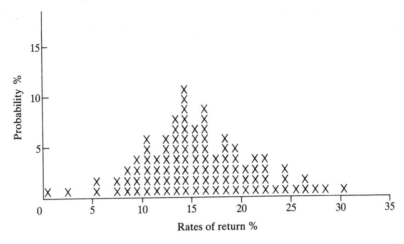

Figure 9.2 Build-up of probability distribution. Each x represents the rate of return from one random selection of values for the project

ties. Approached in the right way, however, it should be possible to form some view of the range of values and probabilities. Indeed, when discussing the planning of a project a manager's response may well be, 'Well I think that it might be x, but it could be as high as y or as low as z.' He has instinctively recognized the uncertainties that exist and has applied his mind to the possible range of values. This should then be built on.

Assume, for example, that one wishes to draw up a distribution curve for the value of annual sales. The value has been provisionally estimated as approaching £3 million per year. Through discussions with the marketing staff it has been established that the likely upper limit to the sales will be £3.8 million and the likely lowest sales value £2.2 million. One has then got to involve the marketing staff in putting probabilities on other values.

After discussion and questioning, a pattern of the probability of different values being achieved might emerge along the following lines:

Lower limit of sales revenue	£2.2 million
There is a 4 per cent chance that it will be between	£2.2 and £2.4 million
There is a 6 per cent chance that it will be between	£2.4 and £2.6 million
There is a 10 per cent chance that it will be between	£2.6 and £2.8 million
There is a 40 per cent chance that it will be between	£2.8 and £3.0 million
There is a 20 per cent chance that it will be between	£3.0 and £3.2 million
There is a 10 per cent chance that it will be between	£3.2 and £3.4 million
There is a 6 per cent chance that it will be between	£3.4 and £3.6 million
There is a 4 per cent chance that it will be between	£3.6 and £3.8 million
Upper limit to sales revenue	£3.8 million

These values can be used to draw up a distribution curve for the sales reve-nue as shown in Figure 9.3. The probability for each of the ranges used above is shown and in many cases this will be adequate. If a curve is re-quired this can be drawn in as shown by the dotted line. The same approach can then be applied to all of the other elements of the project.

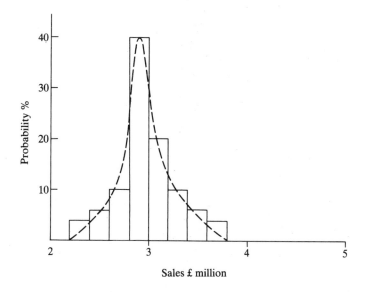

Figure 9.3 Probability distribution of sales

USE OF PROBABILITY DISTRIBUTION CURVES

If a choice has to be made between two major projects, or different ways of carrying out the same project, it may be that the indicated rate of return for each is the same or very close. Where one has built up a probability distribu-tion curve for each project, these can be compared, so that an assessment can be made of the probability of each project exceeding the indicated rate of re-turn and of falling short of that rate.

If one looks at the information given in Figure 9.4 it can be seen that the probability of Project A exceeding the indicated rate of return is much high-er than that of Project B, whereas Project B has a higher probability of fall-ing short of the indicated rate of return and a lower probability of exceeding it. On that basis Project A would be the more desirable.

In Figure 8.1 in Chapter 8, where two similar curves were shown, it can also demonstrate whether one project is more certain, i.e. involves less risk, than the other, even though the balance of probabilities is the same. The flatter the distribution curve then the greater the variability of the possible outcomes.

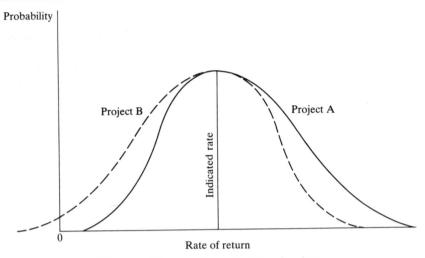

Figure 9.4 Comparable profitability of projects

Sensitivity analysis

While probability analysis gives an overview of the variability of possible outcomes and their probability, it has not really come to terms with the 'What if . . . ?' type of question. The use of sensitivity analysis does enable one to look at individual aspects of a project and answer that sort of question.

Like probability analysis, it requires one to go back to the individual elements that make up a project. These can then be built into a model using a computer spreadsheet. Taking all the most likely values, one can then calculate the most likely rate of return that would emerge. What can then be done is to take a single element of the project, say labour costs, and introduce changes in that value. For example, if they are 10 per cent greater than allowed for in the project planning, what effect would this have on the rate of return? This approach can be used to answer specific 'What if . . . ?' questions. It can, however, be used in a more systematic way to draw up a graph which shows how the rate of return changes for given percentage changes in the key elements of that project.

Example 9.2

Goodco plc is considering investing £100,000 in a new computer-controlled machine to sell a new product. It is estimated that the company will sell 12,000 units of the product per year at a price of £11 each. Labour costs are estimated at 35 per cent of sales. Fixed costs (other than depreciation) are estimated at £29,000 per year and variable costs other than labour at 20 per cent of sales. The machine will be depreciated straight line over ten years.

The economic life of the machine is six years, at the end of which it would have a residual value of £10,000. The project would require the investment in working capital of 10 per cent of the annual sales value. The company has a criterion rate of return of 10 per cent, but management also likes to look at the IRR. The current tax rate is 35 per cent and capital allowances 25 per cent on the reducing balance.

The most likely rate of return is shown in Table 9.4, where it can be seen that the NPV using the 10 per cent criterion rate is £14,000 and the actual rate of return is about 14.5 per cent.

Let us now look at some 'What if . . . ?' questions. Table 9.5 deals with the question of price and answers the question 'What if the price is only £10 per unit instead of the forecast £11, with those costs expressed as percentages remaining the same percentage of the new sales value?' Table 9.6 then looks at the effect of fixed costs being £32,000 instead of £29,000, while Table 9.7 looks at the effect of labour costs rising to 38% of sales. Table 9.8 looks at the effect of the cost of the machine rising to £110,000, and Table 9.9 is based upon sales of only 11,000 units instead of the forecast 12,000 units.

The examples in Tables 9.5 to 9.9 each deal with a specific aspect of the project, and in those cases where the revised values would produce a negative NPV using the 10 per cent discount rate management would have to make some judgement of the probability of the eventuality occurring.

FORMAL ASSESSMENT

The questions posed so far were quite specific and dealt with just one change. A more formal system for assessing the sensitivity of the rate of return can be devised. In Figure 9.5 it can be seen that in the project illustrated the most likely rate of return is 10 per cent. If the value of factor A (let us say direct labour costs) is increased by 10 per cent, 20 per cent and 30 per cent with all the other factors remaining constant, the effect of those changes on the rate of return are seen at a^1, a^2 and a^3. If the labour costs are then reduced by similar percentages, the resulting increases in the rate of return are shown at a^4, a^5 and a^6.

If the points a^1 to a^6 are now connected together by a curve, this shows the rate of return that would result from any percentage change in factor A, within the limits illustrated. If this process is repeated for the other key factors for the project, the relative sensitivity of the rate of return to changes in any one of those factors is clearly seen. For example, the rate of return is much more sensitive to changes in factor C than for factor B.

This identification of relative sensitivity enables management:

1. To identify at the appraisal stage those elements in the project which require the closest scrutiny.

Table 9.4 Example 9.2: most likely rate of return

Year	0	1	2	3	4	5	6	7	8
	£000s								
Sales: 000 units		12.0	12.0	12.0	12.0	12.0	12.0		
Price per unit (£)		11.0	11.0	11.0	11.0	11.0	11.0		
		£000s	£000s	£000s	£000s	£000s	£000s	£000s	£000s
Total sales		132.0	132.0	132.0	132.0	132.0	132.0		
Labour costs: 35% of sales		46.2	46.2	46.2	46.2	46.2	46.2		
Fixed costs		29.0	29.0	29.0	29.0	29.0	29.0		
Depreciation		10.0	10.0	10.0	10.0	10.0	10.0		
Variable costs		26.4	26.4	26.4	26.4	26.4	26.4		
Total costs		111.6	111.6	111.6	111.6	111.6	111.6		
Profit		20.4	20.4	20.4	20.4	20.4	20.4		
Investment	−100.0								
Operating cash flow		30.4	30.4	30.4	30.4	30.4	30.4		
Tax @ 35%			−10.6	−10.6	−10.6	−10.6	−10.6	−10.6	
Pool a/c:									
Added	*100.0*								
Capital allowances	*−25.0*	*−18.8*	*−14.1*	*−10.5*	*−7.9*	*−5.9*	*−4.4*	*−3.3*	
Balance	*75.0*	*56.3*	*42.2*	*31.6*	*23.7*	*17.8*	*13.3*	*Nil*	
Tax saved		8.8	6.6	4.9	3.7	2.8	2.1	1.6	1.2
Working capital		−13.2						13.2	
Sale of machine								10.0	
Cash flow	−100.0	26.0	26.3	24.7	23.5	22.5	21.8	14.1	1.2

NPV @ 10% = £14,000
NPV @ 15% = −£1,600
NPV @ 14% = £1,300

Table 9.5 Example 9.2: with the price of £10 per unit[1]

Year	0	1	2	3	4	5	6	7	8
Sales: 000 units		12.0	12.0	12.0	12.0	12.0	12.0		
Price per unit (£)		10.0	10.0	10.0	10.0	10.0	10.0		
	£000s	£000s	£000s	£000s	£000s	£000s	£000s	£000s	£000s
Total sales		120.0	120.0	120.0	120.0	120.0	120.0		
Labour costs: 35% of sales		42.0	42.0	42.0	42.0	42.0	42.0		
Fixed costs		29.0	29.0	29.0	29.0	29.0	29.0		
Depreciation		10.0	10.0	10.0	10.0	10.0	10.0		
Variable costs: 20% of sales		24.0	24.0	24.0	24.0	24.0	24.0		
Total costs		105.0	105.0	105.0	105.0	105.0	105.0		
Profit		15.0	15.0	15.0	15.0	15.0	15.0		
Investment	−100.0								
Operating cash flow		25.0	25.0	25.0	25.0	25.0	25.0		
Tax @ 35%			−8.8	−8.8	−8.8	−8.8	−8.8	−8.8	
Pool a/c:									
Added	*100.0*								
Capital allowances	*−25.0*	*−18.8*	*−14.1*	*−10.5*	*−7.9*	*−5.9*	*−4.4*	*−3.3*	
Balance	*75.0*	*56.3*	*42.2*	*31.6*	*23.7*	*17.8*	*13.3*	*Nil*	
Tax saved		8.8	6.6	4.9	3.7	2.8	2.1	1.6	1.2
Working capital		−12.0						12.0	
Sale of machine								10.0	
Cash flow	−100.0	21.8	22.8	21.2	19.9	19.0	18.3	14.8	1.2

NPV @ 10% = −£1,500[1]

1. As the NPV is negative when the 10 per cent discount rate is used the project would not meet the criterion rate with the price at £10 per unit.

Table 9.6 Example 9.2: with fixed costs of £32,000[1]

Year	0	1	2	3	4	5	6	7	8
Sales: 000 units		12.0	12.0	12.0	12.0	12.0	12.0		
Price per unit (£)		11.0	11.0	11.0	11.0	11.0	11.0		
	£000s	£000s	£000s	£000s	£000s	£000s	£000s	£000s	£000s
Total sales		132.0	132.0	132.0	132.0	132.0	132.0		
Labour costs: 35% of sales		46.2	46.2	46.2	46.2	46.2	46.2		
Fixed costs		32.0	32.0	32.0	32.0	32.0	32.0		
Depreciation		10.0	10.0	10.0	10.0	10.0	10.0		
Variable costs: 20% of sales		26.4	26.4	26.4	26.4	26.4	26.4		
Total costs		114.6	114.6	114.6	114.6	114.6	114.6		
Profit		17.4	17.4	17.4	17.4	17.4	17.4		
Investment	-100.0								
Operating cash flow		27.4	27.4	27.4	27.4	27.4	27.4		
Tax @ 35%			-9.6	-9.6	-9.6	-9.6	-9.6	-9.6	
Pool a/c:									
Added	*100.0*								
Capital allowances	*-25.0*	*-18.8*	*-14.1*	*-10.5*	*-7.9*	*-5.9*	*-4.4*	*-3.3*	
Balance	*75.0*	*56.3*	*42.2*	*31.6*	*23.7*	*17.8*	*13.3*	*Nil*	
Tax saved		8.8	6.6	4.9	3.7	2.8	2.1	1.6	1.2
Working capital		-13.2						13.2	
Sale of machine								10.0	
Cash flow	-100.0	23.0	24.4	22.7	21.5	20.5	19.9	15.2	1.2

NPV @ 10% = £5,100
NPV @ 12% = -£1,200
NPV @ 11% = £1,900

1. It can be seen that the project would still meet the criterion rate if fixed costs rise to £23,000, but the IRR would fall to about 11.5 per cent.

Table 9.7 Example 9.2: with labour costs at 38% of sales[1]

Year	0	1	2	3	4	5	6	7	8
Sales: 000 units		12.0	12.0	12.0	12.0	12.0	12.0		
Price per unit (£)		11.0	11.0	11.0	11.0	11.0	11.0		
	£000s	£000s	£000s	£000s	£000s	£000s	£000s	£000s	£000s
Total sales		132.0	132.0	132.0	132.0	132.0	132.0		
Labour costs: 38% of sales		50.2	50.2	50.2	50.2	50.2	50.2		
Fixed costs		29.0	29.0	29.0	29.0	29.0	29.0		
Depreciation		10.0	10.0	10.0	10.0	10.0	10.0		
Variable costs: 20% of sales		26.4	26.4	26.4	26.4	26.4	26.4		
Total costs		115.6	115.6	115.6	115.6	115.6	115.6		
Profit		16.4	16.4	16.4	16.4	16.4	16.4		
Investment	−100.0								
Operating cash flow		26.4	26.4	26.4	26.4	26.4	26.4		
Tax @ 35%			−9.3	−9.3	−9.3	−9.3	−9.3	−9.3	
Pool a/c:									
Added	*100.0*								
Capital allowances	*−25.0*	*−18.8*	*−14.1*	*−10.5*	*−7.9*	*−5.9*	*−4.4*	*−3.3*	
Balance	*75.0*	*56.3*	*42.2*	*31.6*	*23.7*	*17.8*	*13.3*	*Nil*	
Tax saved		8.8	6.6	4.9	3.7	2.8	2.1	1.6	1.2
Working capital		−13.2						13.2	
Sale of machine								10.0	
Cash flow	−100.0	22.0	23.7	22.1	20.9	20.0	19.3	15.5	1.2

NPV @ 10% = £2,300
NPV @ 11% = −£900

1. This shows that if labour costs rise to 38 per cent of sales the project would just meet the criterion rate, with the actual rate just under 11 per cent.

133

Table 9.8 Example 9.2: with the machine costing £110,000[1]

Year	0	1	2	3	4	5	6	7	8
Sales: 000 units		12.0	12.0	12.0	12.0	12.0	12.0		
Price per unit (£)		11.0	11.0	11.0	11.0	11.0	11.0		
	£000s	£000s	£000s	£000s	£000s	£000s	£000s	£000s	£000s
Total sales		132.0	132.0	132.0	132.0	132.0	132.0		
Labour costs: 35% of sales		46.2	46.2	46.2	46.2	46.2	46.2		
Fixed costs		29.0	29.0	29.0	29.0	29.0	29.0		
Depreciation		11.0	11.0	11.0	11.0	11.0	11.0		
Variable costs: 20% of sales		26.4	26.4	26.4	26.4	26.4	26.4		
Total costs		112.6	112.6	112.6	112.6	112.6	112.6		
Profit		19.4	19.4	19.4	19.4	19.4	19.4		
Investment	–110.0								
Operating cash flow		30.4	30.4	30.4	30.4	30.4	30.4		
Tax @ 35%			–10.6	–10.6	–10.6	–10.6	–10.6	–10.6	
Pool a/c:									
Added	*110.0*								
Capital allowances	*–27.5*	*–20.6*	*–15.5*	*–11.6*	*–8.7*	*–6.5*	*–4.9*	*–4.7*	
Balance	*82.5*	*61.9*	*46.4*	*34.8*	*26.1*	*19.6*	*14.7*	*Nil*	
Tax saved		9.6	7.2	5.4	4.1	3.0	2.3	1.7	1.6
Working capital		–13.2						13.2	
Sale of machine								10.0	
Cash flow	–110.0	26.8	27.0	25.2	23.8	22.8	22.0	14.3	1.6

NPV @ 10% = £6,600
NPV @ 12% = –£300

1. If the cost of the machine was to rise to £110,000 then the project would still meet the criterion rate and would have an IRR of just under 12%.

Table 9.9 Example 9.2: with sales of 11,000 units per year[1]

Year		0	1	2	3	4	5	6	7	8
	£000s	£000s	£000s	£000s	£000s	£000s	£000s	£000s	£000s
Sales: 000 units			11.0	11.0	11.0	11.0	11.0	11.0		
Price per unit (£)			11.0	11.0	11.0	11.0	11.0	11.0		
Total sales			121.0	121.0	121.0	121.0	121.0	121.0		
Labour costs: 35% of sales			42.3	42.3	42.3	42.3	42.3	42.3		
Fixed costs			29.0	29.0	29.0	29.0	29.0	29.0		
Depreciation			10.0	10.0	10.0	10.0	10.0	10.0		
Variable costs: 20% of sales			24.2	24.2	24.2	24.2	24.2	24.2		
Total costs			105.5	105.5	105.5	105.5	105.5	105.5		
Profit			15.5	15.5	15.5	15.5	15.5	15.5		
Investment		−100.0								
Operating cash flow			25.5	25.5	25.5	25.5	25.5	25.5		
Tax @ 35%				*−8.9*	*−8.9*	*−8.9*	*−8.9*	*−8.9*	*−8.9*	
Pool a/c:										
Added		*100.0*								
Capital allowances		*−25.0*	*−18.8*	*−14.1*	*−10.5*	*−7.9*	*−5.9*	*−4.4*	*−3.3*	
Balance		*75.0*	*56.3*	*42.2*	*31.6*	*23.7*	*17.8*	*13.3*	*Nil*	
Tax saved			8.8	6.6	4.9	3.7	2.8	2.1	1.6	1.2
Working capital			−12.1							12.1	
Sale of machine									10.0	
Cash flow		−100.0	22.1	23.1	21.5	20.2	19.3	18.6	14.7	1.2
NPV @ 10% = −£300										

1. This shows that if sales are only 11,000 units per year then the project would not meet the criterion rate.

135

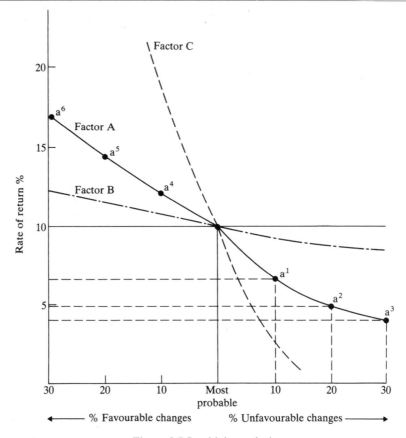

Figure 9.5 Sensitivity analysis

2. To structure the control system when the project is operational, in a way that controls the sensitive factors much more closely.
3. To decide where to probe in detail post-audit work.

As management becomes more scientific in decision-taking it will require a more rigorous quantitative analysis of all aspects of projects, and DCF techniques as used in business must be structured to meet that requirement.

10. *Use of modelling to evaluate risk*

Modelling the firm: key measures

In the business world a model is a simplified overview of the economics of how a firm operates. It takes into account the variables that affect its operations and the relationships between those variables. Taken as a whole they can be used to show what determines the profitability of a business, and the effect on profitability that any changes in the variables would have. At the core of the model of the firm is the relationship between four key measures:

1. The return on capital employed (ROCE)
2. The profit to sales ratio
3. The turnover of capital employed, and
4. The return on equity (ROE).

The relationship between these key measures is shown in Figure 10.1. (The values used in Figure 10.1 are based on the following: the firm has a capital employed (total assets less short-term creditors) of £2 million, and it makes an operating profit (before tax and interest on long-term debt) of £400,000 on sales of £4 million.)

The ROCE is the key measure of management's ability to earn a profit on the funds it has available to use in the business. In the example above the management has available £2 million to use in the business, on which it is able to earn an operating profit of £400,000, therefore it is achieving a ROCE of 20 per cent. Given that ROCE is the key measure of management's effectiveness in running the business, it should be asking 'What determines ROCE?'

Looking at two further ratios, the profit to sales and the turnover of capital employed, one can begin to answer that question. The profit to sales is £400,000 × 100/£4 million, or 10 per cent. The turnover of capital employed measures how effectively management is using the net assets, i.e. the level of sales those net assets can support. In the example the figure is £4 million/ £2 million, or two times the net assets.

With the very simple data used in the above example it can be seen that the ROCE is simply the multiple of the other two values, i.e. the profit to sales ratio and the number of times the capital employed was turned over in the year (ROCE (20%) = Profit/Sales (10%) × Turnover of capital employed (twice)). In other words the ROCE is determined by the profit to sales that is achieved, and the turnover of capital employed—and nothing else. If man-

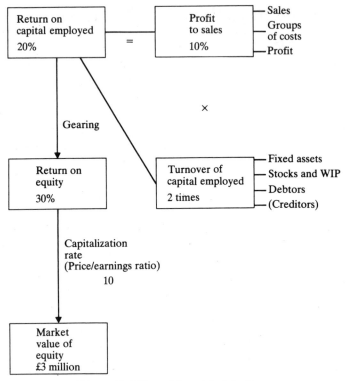

Figure 10.1 Financial model of the firm

agement sets a target of doubling ROCE it will either have to double the profit to sales ratio, or double the turnover of capital employed, or a mixture of the two.

Let us now take a further variable. Let us say that the capital employed is financed by a £1 million 10 per cent loan stock, and £1 million in ordinary shareholders' funds. In other words we have introduced an element of *gearing*. Ignoring tax the operating profit will now be reduced by the interest on the loan, i.e. £400,000 less £100,000 interest, leaving £300,000 for the ordinary shareholders. On the money that they have invested the ROE will be £300,000 × 100/£1 million, or 30 per cent. In this case gearing has increased the ROE from the 20 per cent it would have been had the company been entirely financed by ordinary shareholders' funds, to 30 per cent where half of the company is financed by the 10 per cent loan.

The relationships that have been looked at so far are common to any business and should form the starting point for any analysis of profitability. The next step is to ask oneself 'What determines the profit to sales ratio?' and 'What determines the turnover of capital employed ratio?' The profit to sales ratio is effectively determined by the value of sales and the values of the various groups of cost incurred in that type of business, with the residual element being the profit. If any cost group absorbs a higher proportion of the sales it is likely to do this at the expense of profits. The operating budgets of a business are the way that management tries to plan what these values should be and to use that plan to monitor performance.

Another factor which might be considered when we try to translate these factors into a business model is the variability of the various groups of cost as volume changes. Some of the costs, such as rent and depreciation, will be relatively fixed, whatever the volume of business, whereas others, such as materials, labour and consumables, will tend to increase in line with volume changes. What will be the implication for profit of such differences?

The turnover of capital employed shows the relationship between the capital employed and sales. Remember that one way of looking at capital employed is in terms of net assets, and that the major items one will see in net assets will be investments in fixed assets, in stocks and work in progress, and in debtors. Since it is net assets that we are talking about, the value of these items is offset by short-term creditors (those payable within one year). There are factors which limit the use that can be made of short-term credit, not least from the business's own point of view, since too great a reliance on the use of short-term credit adds to the risk of business failure. If one accepts that, then the real task of management is to control the investment in fixed assets, stocks and work in progress together with debtors in relation to the level of sales. If there are proper stock control and credit control systems operating within the business then ratios of stocks and debtors to sales can test whether those systems are operating effectively and give the appropriate signals to management. Since both items are short-term investments of money, then corrective action will soon begin to bite if things move in the wrong direction.

In the case of fixed assets wrong decisions cannot be corrected so readily. The investment in such assets is made for a number of years and cannot be changed easily. The point at which decisions on the value and composition of fixed assets must be made is *before* the investment is made, which is of course why we need investment appraisal systems and capital budgeting as a whole.

Ratios should not be looked at independently as is so often the case, but should be linked together to show the core of the business model as shown in Figure 10.1. Not only are the ratios linked together in the way that is shown in that figure, but there are also economic trade-offs at the operating end. Take the subject of this book, investment in new projects. Some of these investments may be in new advanced technology which will make the business more capital intensive. This will reduce the turnover of capital employed. On the other hand, the purpose of such investment is to reduce costs.

So which cost groups will be reduced and what effect will that have on the profit to sales ratio? When the two effects are combined within the model used so far, then will it increase or reduce the ROCE? The function of investment appraisal techniques is to try and answer that quite basic question before the company commits more money to that investment.

If the model is to be taken further then the relationships between the various operational factors which govern the business will have to be looked at. These will vary from business to business so no common framework can be established. Some of the factors that are likely to be looked at are, however, the sensitivity of volume to price changes, how costs will change as volume changes, effects of scale when adding to the business, and so on. These factors as they are determined can be added to the basic framework that has been established so far.

The market value of the equity will be the earnings available to ordinary shareholders times the price/earnings ratio. In the case illustrated, if the shares are traded on 10 times earnings then the market value of the equity will be £300,000 × 10 = £3 million.

Use of modelling in investment appraisal

As was seen in the last chapter which dealt with risk and uncertainty, management has problems in making decisions because of the uncertain nature of the data presented with the proposal. In sensitivity analysis it was suggested that one way to provide more in-depth information to appraise an investment is to ask 'What if?' type of questions. This involved looking at individual elements of the project and assuming changes in the values that might occur, and calculating the effect of those changes on the rate of return. If there is available a model of how the business operates and the variables have been identified then that process can be made more effective.

For government use the Treasury has available a model showing how the nation's economy as a whole should work, and this model can be used by economists outside government. In a large business it might be the case that a model covering all of the company's activities has been evolved over the years. When major investment decisions are required then the consequences of the various alternatives that might be under consideration can be tested, as well as a range of variables at different stages of the model.

Until recent years the use of models in this way would almost certainly have been confined to the very large organization which had the resources to research and build them. But modelling is now within the grasp of organizations of almost any size. The advent of the mini and personal computer and word processors enables individuals with no programming skills to construct fairly straightforward models for individual investment projects using the appropriate software.

Spreadsheets

A spreadsheet is a grid or matrix of cells. In a typical spreadsheet they may be arranged in 50 or 60 columns and over 200 rows. Each cell within the spreadsheet can carry a description, e.g. 'Sales', it can carry a number, e.g. 1 million, or it can be a function. If for example the 1 million represented units of sales and they are sold at £10 each, then in the spreadsheet this could be shown as follows:

	COLUMN 1	COLUMN 2
ROW A Sales:	Units	1,000,000
ROW B	Price (per unit)	£10
ROW C	Value (a) × (b)	£10,000,000

In this illustration, in column 1 we have descriptions, i.e. Sales in terms of Units, Price, etc. In column 2 we have values, e.g. in cell A2 (i.e. ROW A/COLUMN 2) the number of units sold, in cell B2 the price at which the units are sold, and in cell C2 the function A2 × B2 and the result of that function, i.e. a sales value of £10,000,000.

With the flexibility of spreadsheets that can be used on quite simple computers the above example can be expanded into a quite complex model. As far as investment appraisal is concerned the capacity of a spreadsheet can accommodate all the years for any likely project in the columns, and the number of rows provide adequate space to build up the basic data for a project, remembering that the function outlined above can operate between any pair of cells. For example, if the operating cash flow for year 3 is in cell F5, and we are calculating the extra tax payable in Row G, then since tax is payable in the year following that in which profits are earned, the function in cell G6 would be F5 × 0.35 which would give us the tax payable in year 4.

In fact nearly all of the computations of present value or rates of return used in this book have been carried out on a simple computer/word processor with a quite basic spreadsheet program. Such programs are also likely to have an inbuilt NPV function and a 'Breakeven' function which cuts down the computation.

To illustrate this let us look at the data for Exercise 5.4 from Chapter 5. Look on each description and set of figures as occupying a single cell. The relationships between those cells are as follows:

1. *Cost of plant.* This is given in the text.
2. *Operating cash flows.* This has been done outside the printed solution but could equally have been incorporated into the spreadsheet, as it is selling price × units of sales = total sales value, then, − fixed overheads other than depreciation − total variable costs (variable costs per unit × units of sales) = operating cash flows.

3. *Tax at 35%.* This is the operating cash flow for the previous year × the tax rate and is a negative figure.

4. *Pool account.* This and the next three lines compute the capital allowances. 'Added' shows how much the cost of plant etc. adds to the pool account; 'Capital allowances' shows how much is claimed in that year, and with the current system operating in the UK, will in the first year be the added value × 25 per cent, and in the following years the previous year's balance × 25 per cent; and 'Balance' is the previous years balance – the capital allowances claimed in the year. Provision will have to be made at the end of the project to bring the total capital allowances to the difference between the cost and the sale value of the plant by a + or – adjustment.

5. *Tax saved.* This is the tax saving through capital allowances and is the previous year's claim for capital allowances × the tax rate of 35 per cent.

6. *Working capital.* This is given in the exercise details, but could also be based on the increase or decrease in sales value in the specified years × a given percentage.

7. *Sale of plant.* This is given in the exercise details and is taken into account when computing 4 above.

8. *Cash flow.* This is a straight addition of all of the values used other than those which are inserted to compute the pool account details.

The NPV function in the program has then been used to compute the present value using the 10 per cent discount rate. For completeness the PV factors and the present values (cash flow for that year × present value factors for that year) have been included. This is not necessary as the NPV can be computed directly from the cash flows. If one wanted to find the IRR for the project then one could use different discount rates as has been done in Exercise 5.8. There several rates have been used until the rate has been bracketed. At a discount rate of 14 per cent the NPV is –£12,400 and at 13 per cent the NPV is £17,900, so the IRR is about half way between those two rates, i.e. approximately 13.5 per cent.

Use of spreadsheets in analysing sensitivity

As a first step, all of those values mentioned in 2 above can be set out individually in the spreadsheet starting with the volume of sales in units, and the various steps to working out the operating cash flow built in. It may be that management wants these set out differently to reflect the nature of the business. In practice this means that it may be desirable to identify the various cost groups, such as direct labour, and provide sub-totals for fixed and variable cost.

The 'What if . . . ?' questions can now be answered by holding other values constant and simply changing the value for the one that is being questioned. The NPV and, if required, the IRR can then be computed for the changed values.

This was done in Example 9.2 where the individual items that make up the project were defined as:

1. Sales in number of units
2. Price per unit
3. Labour cost as a percentage of sales
4. Fixed overheads
5. Depreciation
6. Variable costs.

These values have enabled the total cost and profit to be computed prior to looking at the cash flow consequences. The example then proceeds to compute the cash flows and NPV and IRR in the same way as before, the operating cash flow being the profit for the year plus the depreciation charged for that year.

Example 9.2 then looked at the effects of changes in some of those values. This was done simply by changing the value or function for that item (for example, the labour cost value is the function sales value × the stated percentage).

With more sophisticated equipment and programming one can build up a more sophisticated model for the appraisal of projects. Do remember, however, that the appraisal is only as good as the data that has been put into the program. No amount of sophistication is going to help if the basic budgeting for the project is faulty, but this sort of approach can help to identify limits of changes in values of the elements of the project that could be related to the possible variability of the basic data, and that affects rates of return.

Long-term financial planning

Setting the strategy

Long-term financial planning is part of the overall strategic planning touched upon in Chapter 1 and must be considered in that context. The long-term planning process begins with an appraisal of the likely trends in the environment within which the business operates over the planning period. What that planning period will be depends upon what type of business the firm operates. In nuclear power generation that planning period might stretch over several decades. In areas where technological change is rapid, whether in the product or the way that it is marketed etc., then the planning period will be relatively short—perhaps over only four or five years.

Having determined the likely changes in the environment then management has to develop a strategy that will enable the business to exploit those changes the most effectively. In the process of developing that overall strategy it will be necessary to make strategic decisions about the basic operational areas of the business. A logical sequence for making these decisions would be the following:

1. The range of products or services: how is that range to alter over the planning period?
2. When the range of products has been identified then the areas where research and development expenditure has to be directed will have been identified.
3. The marketing strategy. How the product is to be marketed, pricing policy, etc., will be determined at this stage. At the end of the process management should have some idea of the likely volumes of its product that will be sold.
4. The production strategy. There are various approaches to how the goods or services are to be provided. A high-risk strategy of expensive, cost-effective equipment, specific to the product might be adopted, or a low-risk one using more versatile equipment that could be used for other products but with higher costs. Decisions may also have to be made regarding securing the sources of materials etc. that it needs.
5. In developing the production strategy management will most likely identify areas where new expenditures on physical assets, such as buildings, plant and equipment, will be required, and the general nature of such requirements.
6. Businesses need more than physical resources. They need human skills

144

in both the workforce and management, and at this stage the skills required to meet the strategic goals of the business would be identified.
7. The financial strategy. Where is the money that is required to meet all of the identified needs to come from? Decisions here will deal with the continuing balance between loan finance and owner's finance (or the debt/equity ratio), what the dividend policy is to be if we are dealing with a company, and so on.
8. Other matters that would be dealt with are organizational development, the reaction of the business with the environment (i.e. its 'green' policy), what role it is to play in the community, and so on.

ASSESSING THE ACCEPTABILITY OF THE STRATEGY

Having developed such a strategy, management must then test it to see whether or not it is acceptable in financial terms. This means that the plan will be turned into financial data so that the likely levels of profit and the overall investment values can be determined to see, first of all, whether that would represent an adequate rate of return on the capital employed, and secondly, whether that rate of return, looked at from the investor's and potential investor's points of view, would give them an adequate return in terms of dividend and capital growth.

This is a crucial stage. The strategy proposed is almost certain to require the raising of new capital and management has to recognize that investors are not philanthropists. Indeed, much of the new investment will be made by the trustees of pension funds and charities who have a positive duty to secure the best return for their clients. If there are numerous opportunities in the market-place to invest money with an overall return in excess of, say, 15 per cent per year, then if the proposed strategy is only likely to provide an overall return of, say, 10 per cent, then it is unlikely to be able to raise the capital that it will need. The ultimate test of whether a proposed strategy should be adopted must be whether it will offer the 'going rate' of the marketplace. If it does not then the strategy must be rethought until an acceptable one is produced.

Example 11.1

Targo plc has a capital employed of £1 million with a financing policy and profits as shown in the first column of Table 11.1 on page 146. The board has decided not to call upon shareholders for additional cash except through retention of profits, as major shareholders would be unable to subscribe to a rights issue. It is proposed to distribute 60 per cent of earnings year by year, and as the value of shareholders' funds increase as a consequence of the 40 per cent retained profit, borrowings will be raised in minimum £100,000 issues to maintain broadly the 50:50 ratio between shareholders' and borrowed funds. The forecast after-tax cost of borrowed money is 4 per cent. Management's target return on capital employed is 8 per cent after tax.

Table 11.1 Example 11.1: overall return to shareholders

Years	1 £000s	2 £000s	3 £000s	4 £000s	5 £000s	6 £000s	7 £000s	8 £000s	9 £000s	10 £000s
Capital employed	1,000	1,024	1,049	1,075	1,201	1,230	1,260	1,291	1,423	1,457
Profit (after tax)	80	82	84	86	96	98	102	104	114	117
Loans	500	500	500	500	600	600	600	600	700	700
Cost of interest	20	20	20	20	24	24	24	24	28	28
Profit for shareholders	60	62	64	66	72	74	78	80	86	89
Dividends	36	37	38	40	43	44	47	48	52	53
Retained profits	24	25	26	26	29	30	31	32	34	36
Net borrowing	—	—	—	—	100	—	—	—	100	—
Valuation of equity if price/earnings ratio is 20	1,200	1,240	1,280	1,320	1,440	1,480	1,560	1,600	1,720	1,780

1. Calculation of the overall return to shareholders is given in Table 11.1.
2. Valuation of shareholders' return:
   (a) Purchase of a 10 per cent interest in the shares at end of year 1 would cost £120,000.
   (b) If held for 9 years to the end of year 10 the return would be:

Year	Dividends £000s	Capital gain £000s
2	3.7	—
3	3.8	—
4	4.0	—
5	4.3	—
6	4.4	—
7	4.7	—
8	4.8	—
9	5.2	—
10	5.3	58 (Realized 178 less cost 120)
	40.2	58

   (c) The equivalent gross dividend total is 40,200 × 100/75 = 53,600. Total return 53,600 + 58,000 capital gains provides an overall pre-tax return of 111,600. To find the actual rate of return on the investment one could use DCF on the basis dealt with in Chapter 7.
3. The after-tax discounted rate of return (assuming that the shareholder pays tax on income of 25 per cent but that the capital gains would take him or her into the 40 per cent rate, and ignoring indexation) is given in Table 11.2.

It can thus be seen that, based upon the assumption built into the long-term plan, an investment in Targo plc would provide the investor with a return of just over 6 per cent after tax over the nine year period. If the market offers, say, 8 per cent after tax to investors, the proposed plan should not be accepted.

Relationship between long-term planning and financial criteria used in investment appraisal

In the various stages of the long-term planning process dealt with above there are two which are highly relevant to investment appraisal. In point 5 on page 144 it was seen that areas for new investment in plant and equipment will have been identified. It follows that when investment decisions are being looked at on a year-by-year basis the selection should conform to the general pattern that has been laid down.

147

Table 11.2 Example 11.1: after-tax discounted rate of return

Year[2]	Net dividends £000s	Sale of shares £000s	Capital gains tax £000s	Cash flow £000s	PV factors 6%	Present value £000s
1	3.7	—	—	3.7	0.943	3.49
2	3.8	—	—	3.8	0.890	3.38
3	4.0	—	—	4.0	0.840	3.36
4	4.3	—	—	4.3	0.792	3.41
5	4.4	—	—	4.4	0.747	3.29
6	4.7	—	—	4.7	0.705	3.31
7	4.8	—	—	4.8	0.665	3.19
8	5.2	—	—	5.2	0.627	3.26
9	5.3	178.0	−23.2[1]	160.1	0.592	94.78
						121.47

1. Based on gain of £58 × 40% tax.
2. Discount years equivalent to years 2 to 10 in part 2 above.

In point 7 on page 145 it was seen that the financial strategy requires a decision on the mix of funds to be used to finance the business. The balance between debt and equity will influence the cost of capital as will be seen in the next chapter. In general, the after-tax cost of borrowing money is likely to be less than the opportunity cost of equity, so the more debt that is used in relation to equity, the lower is likely to be the *average* cost of capital. This decision will therefore be a major determinant of the criterion rate to be used in the selection process, if the cost of capital is to be used for that purpose.

Manager and investor attitudes to the use of long-term debt have changed radically in recent years and, of course, may change equally in the future. Some of the recent leveraged (highly geared) management buyouts and the philosophy of 'junk' bonds have seen the use of debt rise to unprecedented levels. But it might only need one or two spectacular failures in this area for there to be a reaction against such high levels of gearing.

Hopefully a more positive approach will be taken to establish the criterion rate. As seen above, the test of whether a proposed strategy is acceptable depends upon whether or not it meets the long-term overall return demanded in the market. The rate of return on capital employed on which that assessment is made is an indicator of what must be achieved in the future, and all new investment should meet that rate. As part of its overall long-term planning process management should use the data on which it is working to set a criterion rate or rates that will meet its requirements.

Constraints

There are many governmental and quasi-governmental organizations which may be in a position to impose constraints on how a business operates, and the board of directors themselves may, to protect the company's interests, set criteria for the behaviour of the business. These constraints would include:

1. *Relations with staff.* Specific practices in relationship to employees may be laid down, or guidelines set out.
2. *Trading practices.* Guidelines on how the business is to be carried on within the framework of the various legislative requirements in this area should be clearly set out.
3. *Health and safety.* This is an increasingly important field and one which may well constrain the way in which a project can be carried out.
4. *Environmental issues.* These may be enshrined in law, but management may also wish to set out the company's attitudes and practices.

This process of formulating strategies and testing them against desired levels of profit is shown in Figure 11.1.

Need for a portfolio of activities

It has already been stated that when selecting projects in terms of profitability, some consideration must be given to securing a mix of projects that do not all have the major part of their cash flows arising in distant years in time, leaving early years bereft of both profit flows and cash flows. The products on which many projects are based themselves have a life-cycle—short for some, long for others. Here, once again, the aim of management should be to select a mix of products which gives a reasonably smooth trend in profits.

This can be seen in Figure 11.2. The individual product has a period of early growth to reach maturity. The mature period may last some time, but eventually the competitiveness of that product is likely to decline and it becomes less and less profitable as shown in (a). A mix of products, all in their mature stage and which are all likely to start declining at the same time as shown in (b), is going to lead to severe problems for the company as it goes through that period of decline. Ideally, management should try and maintain a mix of products all at differing stages of their life-cycles as in (c), so that there is a stream of new products taking the place of those which are fading out, thus securing continuity for the business.

How to secure the long-term future of the business

In the author's view the long-term future of the business can only be secured as follows:

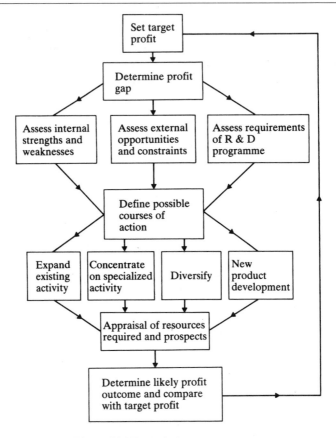

Figure 11.1 Formulating corporate strategy

1. By a clear statement of the strategy that the company is to follow over its planning time horizon.
2. Through that strategy by ensuring a mix of activities that will provide a steady growth in profit and cash.
3. By ensuring, through its planning processes, that the liquidity of the business is maintained.
4. Within the framework and constraints established, by ensuring that there is an effective investment appraisal system for the selection of projects.

Which appraisal technique to use

In the past there has been much argument about the merits of the DCF or internal rate of return and the net present value methods. Much of this

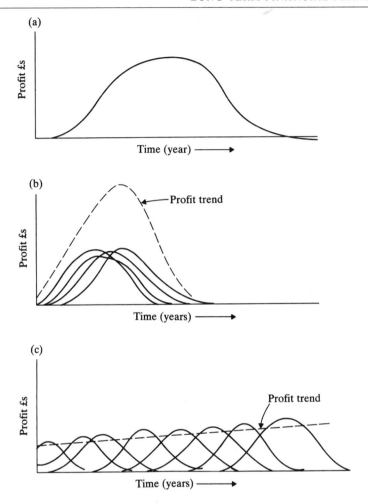

Figure 11.2 Product life: (a) product life-cycle; (b) wrong product mix; (c) right product mix

argument has been based on the use of the NPV on its own as the basis for the selection of projects on the lines that the greater the NPV added to the business, the better the project. But, as stated earlier, this basis takes no account of the money that has had to be invested to earn that NPV. NPV on its own may well give quite different rankings to projects to those given by the rate of return method. But if NPV is used in conjunction with calculating the profitability index as suggested in Chapter 2, then the two methods should give broadly the same results.

The argument has also been centred on what cash can earn *after* it is released from a project. But this is really irrelevant. What one has to measure is what that particular project could afford to pay for the money invested in it, and this is its real measure of profitability.

The argument is really academic today. Even the least sophisticated computer with the right software is capable of calculating both the NPV and the DCF or internal rate of return. Management should therefore have both of these values available to use.

12. The cost of capital and capital budgeting

As managers of the business on behalf of the general body of shareholders, the board of directors should have two principal objectives in mind in relation to their financial policy. These are:

1. To ensure that the return earned on the long-term funds (or net assets) employed in the business is maintained at the maximum sustainable in the long term.
2. To arrange the way in which the financing requirements of the business are met so that the overall long-term return to shareholders, in terms of both income and capital appreciation, is maximized within given risk constraints.

Investment appraisal is intimately concerned with the first of these objectives. Each time it is proposed to commit a part of the cash of a business to a specific use, DCF can be used to measure the return that that cash would earn. This should lead to a process of selection of projects that should eliminate the less profitable ones.

The second of these objectives is not so directly related to DCF. The link between the two lies in the fact that the decision taken on the relationship between debt and equity will, as already outlined, influence the cost of capital to the business thus setting an absolute minimum acceptable rate of return.

Gearing

Let us look at the way in which methods of financing a company can affect the rate of return to the ordinary shareholders—the gearing effect. A simple illustration of this is shown in Table 12.1. This assumes that a new business requires a total investment of £100,000 capital, and it should earn before interest and tax £15,000 per year. The table examines two possible methods of financing the £100,000 capital requirement. The first of these relies entirely on raising cash from ordinary shareholders, i.e. with no gearing at all. The second alternative uses a combination of different sources of capital. The effect of the latter financing choice is to more than double the rate of return on the ordinary shareholders' funds (ignoring tax).

This is illustrated in Figure 12.1. In the 'all equity' choice the whole of the £100,000 capital is in the form of ordinary shares, and the return on that capital is 15 per cent. In the 'mixed capital' structure the segments of capital provided by the various sources are shown in their sequence. The debenture

Table 12.1 Effect of gearing on the return to the ordinary shareholders

All the capital provided by ordinary shareholders		Mixture of different sources of funds	
	£		£
Ordinary share capital	100,000	6% Debentures	40,000
		7% Preference shares	30,000
		Ordinary share capital	30,000
		Total capital	100,000
Operating profit	15,000	Operating profit	15,000
		Debenture interest	2,400
		Profit before tax	12,600
Profit available to ordinary shareholders	15,000	Preference dividend	2,100
		Profit available to ordinary shareholders	10,500
Return on equity	15%	Return on equity: 10,500/30,000 × 100 =	35%

carries a rate of 6 per cent and will absorb the area of operating profit shown. In normal times the preference dividend of 7 per cent will have to be paid because until this is done no dividend can be paid to the ordinary shareholders. This will absorb its appropriate part of the operating profit. All of the remaining profit belongs to the ordinary shareholders and in effect the unshaded parts of the operating profit above the two other sources of capital swing over and add to the rate of return that the ordinary shareholders' funds earn.

It follows from Figure 12.1 that as long as management can earn more than the cost of attracting finance from other people when it puts that money to work in the business, then the higher it gears up its capital structure and the higher will be the return on equity. If it earns less than the cost of those sources of finance, e.g. in the case illustrated, if it only earned 6 per cent on total capital employed, then gearing will work in the opposite direction. When a company has gearing the gearing will not only affect the absolute return on equity, but also the rate at which the return on equity will change. That is to say it will go up faster and come down faster than the rate of return on total capital employed.

Inherent in this is the risk that gearing imposes on the business. It now has fixed legal commitments to pay interest and repay loans and perhaps other obligations which it cannot avoid. If it fails to meet these, then lenders will take whatever legal action is open to them to recover their money, e.g. in the case of debentures assets will have been charged under the terms of the debenture and the lender will appoint a receiver who takes over the assets charged and sells them to pay off the loan.

154

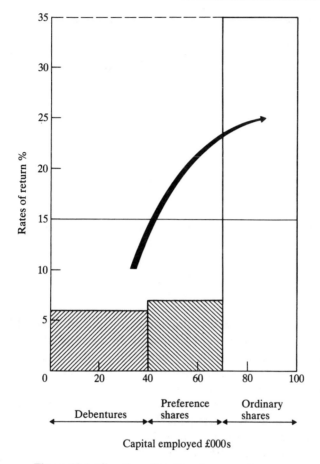

Figure 12.1 Allocation of earnings in a geared company

Gearing, therefore, has another side to it. The higher the gearing the higher the risk of business failure through being unable to meet loan commitments. Management must therefore select a combination of debt and equity which balances the beneficial effects of gearing against those higher risks.

BALANCE BETWEEN DIFFERENT TYPES OF FUNDS

The importance of gearing from the point of view of DCF is that once management has defined its policy on the type and extent of gearing for the company, the approximate proportion of each source of funds can be seen. This does not mean that there will not be deviations from that norm. The raising of capital is not so precise an operation as that. Borrowing money and rais-

155

ing additional capital from shareholders will usually only be undertaken in fairly large tranches, each of which can disturb the relationship in the short term. What it does mean, however, is that over the long term the balance of funds will tend to converge on that norm. If the current fund raising is, say, in the form of additional borrowing, this may temporarily increase the proportion of capital funded by borrowing. This means that the next requirement to raise capital will probably be met by shareholders. Only in the case of retained profits is the accrual of capital likely to be a continuous accretion.

Cost of different sources of funds

Given that the fundamental financing decision outlined earlier has been taken and that there are unlikely to be any further major changes in the basic relationship between borrowed and equity funds, it is possible to project the likely average cost of capital to the business. This will involve estimating the likely cost of each source and calculating the *weighted average cost* for that mix of funds to be used in the business. The weights to be used in this process are the actual or prospective proportion of the funds derived from each of the sources. The cost of those sources is the measure of the return that must be paid to or imputed to the providers of those funds.

BORROWED FUNDS
The cost of borrowed money is usually clear cut as the terms of the loan will specify the rates that have to be paid. The only problem that might arise is where a floating rate is paid, i.e. where the rate depends on, for example, the London Inter Bank Rate (LIBOR). The interest that is paid is relievable for tax so that a loan at 10 per cent will have an after-tax cost of 6.5 per cent, where the tax rate is 35 per cent.

SHAREHOLDERS' FUNDS
Measuring the cost of shareholders' funds is not so straightforward. While preference shares have a fixed rate of dividend which can be used to measure their cost, with ordinary shares this is not the case, and a different approach will be needed.

The cost of preference share capital after tax is the stated dividend rate, since under UK tax law that is the amount that will be paid to the shareholders in cash, and they will receive a tax credit to cover their basic tax liability. In measuring the cost of ordinary share capital the rate of dividend paid is not relevant, since this would imply that where a company had a policy of paying no dividends its cost of equity capital would be zero. Also one must look further than the book value of the issued ordinary shares. All profits and gains that are not distributed belong to the ordinary shareholders, so it is the cost of the *total* ordinary shareholders' funds that is relevant.

One way of determining that cost is to look at what the shareholder could earn on that money if it was in his pocket and available to invest, i.e. the concept of the opportunity cost of that money. Or one could look at one of the financial models to calculate that cost. For example:

If k = cost of equity
  d = the dividend per share
  p = the current share price
  g = the expected growth

then k can be expressed as:

$$k = \frac{d+g}{p}$$

As can be seen, any method used to evaluate the cost of equity is likely to require some element of judgement about the future growth rate.

AVERAGE COST OF CAPITAL *v.* MARGINAL COST

Many business decisions are made on the basis of marginal cost, so why not in the case of the cost of capital? If, for example, this year we are going to spend £10 million on a new building, and finance this by the issue of an 11 per cent debenture, why not use the cost of that debenture? If the investment on the building will earn 8 per cent after tax, it would more than meet the after-tax cost of the loan of 7.15 per cent (11 per cent less tax at 35 per cent). But as mentioned earlier in this chapter, because the fund raising this year has been via borrowed money, it is highly probable that next year's investments will have to be financed by equity in order to maintain the norm in the mix of funds used. Various studies have estimated that the cost of equity is likely to be some 10–11 per cent, so a project earning 9.5 per cent next year would be turned down, as it would not meet the marginal cost of the capital used. A selection method that accepted a return of 8 per cent one year and rejected one of 9.5 per cent the following year would mean that management is not maximizing the overall return on the investments that it is making. This is why one must look at the ongoing average cost of capital to the business.

It is also useful to reiterate what was said at the beginning of this book. A business draws its capital from a number of different sources to provide a general pool of funds. Out of this pool it allocates amounts as and when required for various projects. Any particular use of funds on a project cannot, however, be identified with the particular source from which it came. Each source contributes to the general pool of funds, or what is generally called the capital employed. Out of this general pool management will allocate funds to specific projects. Whether the funds that are allocated to a project were originally raised by means of a debenture or from retained profits, for example, is purely fortuitous.

There may be exceptional cases where the marginal cost is appropriate. A property investment company may well raise finance which is specific to each building. Here there is such a close relationship between the investment and the way in which it is financed that it may be more appropriate to use the actual funds used. Similarly, if we are dealing with a specific investment overseas, where political and economic considerations necessitate raising funds in a particular way, the cost of the actual funds might be considered. However, one would always have to take into consideration how that method of finance might affect the business as a whole.

Such cases must be dealt with on their merits, not losing sight of the effect the decision may have on the future raising of capital for the company or group as a whole. In any case, a marginal rate that is less than the average rate should not be used since projects earning less than the average rate will lower the level of profitability of the business as a whole.

WEIGHTED AVERAGE COST OF CAPITAL

When the decisions have been made on the balance of funding for the business and the after-tax cost of each of the sources has been identified, these factors can be brought together to calculate the weighted average cost as shown in Table 12.2.

Capital budgeting

PROJECTS WITH A NIL RATE OF RETURN

If the criterion rate of return is to be based upon the cost of capital then when management has determined the average weighted cost of capital to the business, it must then determine the relationship that should exist between that cost and the criterion rate or rates. This relationship must take into account those projects with a nil rate of return as well as building in differentials for different levels of risk.

The projects that compete for capital available for investment may include some projects to which no rate of return can be ascribed, such as those dealt with on page 11. Although these projects have no rate of return it is necessary for the business to invest money in them for it to remain in business. The remaining projects must earn a rate of return in excess of the average cost of capital so that when *all* projects are taken into account they more than cover that cost.

Example 12.1

The board of directors of Trelawney plc are considering the overall allocation of funds to new investment for the following year. The proposals sub-

Table 12.2 Calculating the weighted average cost of capital

Source of funds	Book value of funds £m	% of total %	After-tax cost %	Weighted amount
10% Debentures	1.0	14.29	6.5	92.885
12% Unsecured loan	2.0	28.57	7.8	222.846
7% Preference shares	0.5	7.14	7.0	49.980
Ordinary share capital	2.0 ⎫	50.00	10.0	500.00
Reserves	1.5 ⎭			
	7.0	100.00		865.711
Weighted average cost of capital	8.66%			

mitted for consideration are those shown in the first three columns of Table 12.3. The average weighted cost of capital to the company is 8.5 per cent.

Each of the projects included in Table 12.3 that has a rate of return, shows a rate in excess of the cost of capital. The rate of return on the proposed investments as a whole, however, falls below the cost of capital by 0.52 per cent. Clearly if the schedule of investments was to be approved as it stands, the earnings from this mix of projects would fall below the cost of capital, and thus reduce profitability.

Taking into account those investments that may be required by law, management must define its policy towards the commitment of funds to non-earning projects, and decide what proportion of the cash available will be devoted to this purpose. Once defined, the basis for the criterion rate of return will be that the average return on the investments as a whole will exceed the cost of capital. Where management is fixing the criterion rate through the long-term planning process then the rate determined must allow for the investment in 'nil' rate of return projects.

MORE THAN ONE CRITERION RATE OF RETURN

Management should then consider whether just one criterion rate should be used or whether other rates should be used for projects which carry a greater risk. Among the projects shown in Table 12.3, for example, the investment listed under 'Launch new product' will carry a higher risk than the other projects which are concerned with replacing machines or providing more sophisticated ones. That difference in risk might be emphasized by classifying projects according to the perceived amount of risk and setting higher criterion rates for those with the highest risks. This is a conservative approach to risk and almost amounts to trying to avoid it as far as possible, but as stat-

Table 12.3 Capital budget, Trelawney plc

Item	Amount of funds required £000s	After-tax return %	Weighted after-tax return
Automatic conveyor system	1,000	10	10,000
Toilet block	360	Nil	Nil
New product launch:			
Buildings	500		
Plant	620 }	9	11,430
Working capital	150		
Replacing delivery vehicles	100	8.5	850
New canteen	250	Nil	Nil
Machine replacement	1,100	9	9,900
Automatic packing machine	90	12	1,080
Total	4,170		33,260

Average return on projects: 33,260/4,170 = 7.98%

ed in Chapter 8 avoiding risk itself can present problems. So perhaps the best way of dealing with it is through the techniques of probability and sensitivity analysis outlined earlier.

Inflation

In recent decades the economies of countries all over the world have suffered from the effects of inflation to a greater or lesser degree. As far as individual businesses are concerned the effect of inflation, unless properly dealt with in management's decision-making process, is to increase the financing requirement in the same way as an increase in the level of business transacted would require more capital. The concern that management should have, therefore, when making investment decisions based upon the current purchasing power of money, is how inflation will affect the outcome of the project in *real* terms.

If all costs and revenues were inflating at the same rate, then apart from one item, inflation would have no affect on the real rate of return. That one item is capital allowances dealt with on page 43. These (or depreciation in countries other than the UK), are spread over the life of the asset, and the cash flow effects will therefore be reduced in real terms by inflation over the life of the project.

The only way that this could be dealt with in practice is to produce a model of the mix of values typical of that business's projects, build in reductions in the value of capital allowances that would occur under different rates of inflation, and see how the ensuing rates of return differ from that where no inflation is taken into account. These differences could be added to the criterion rate to compensate for the effects of the rate of inflation on capital allowances that is forecast. The great difficulty is to forecast the rate of inflation!

Where components of the project are inflating at rates different to the general rate of inflation then the problem becomes more complex. As a minimum the project costs (and if necessary the parts of the investment required) would need to be broken down into the areas with different inflation rates. The inflation rates assumed would then be applied to each of the areas using the various rates that have been adopted. The tax flows would then be based upon each year's taxable profits, and the total cash flow for each year calculated.

One has now determined each year's cash flow denominated in pounds of the purchasing power for that year. These cash flows would then need to be brought back to pounds of current purchasing power. These could then be discounted in the normal way. The main problem in dealing with inflation is, however, forecasting what the rate of inflation will be in two or three years' time, let alone in ten or twenty years. As stated elsewhere in this book, the future is never certain and this is particularly the case with trying to estimate rates of inflation.

There is one practical problem that can occur. This arises where there is a large land and buildings element involved in the investment for the project, and possibly where there is a large working capital content. Both of these types of investment in a project are released when it comes to an end. As the termination of the project is likely to be many years ahead in time there will be a temptation to relate the associated residual values with their money value at the date of termination. This could lead to the wrong decision being made.

Look at the project shown in Table 12.4. It has an investment made up of £60,000 in plant and equipment and £100,000 in buildings. It has a ten-year life and should generate positive cash flows of £9,000 per year over that period. It is estimated that the market value of the building at the end of the ten-year period will be £300,000. The management has set a target rate of return of 10 per cent. On the face of it, it would appear that the project just meets the 10 per cent criterion rate, since the present value of the future cash flows of £160,305 exceeds the investment of £160,000.

However, if one strips out the building content of the project, we have a project with an investment in plant and machinery of £60,000, and a present value of the future cash flows of only £55,305, i.e. a negative net present value, and one that should, therefore, be rejected. The reason that the project originally seemed to be acceptable was that inflation had been built in to the residual value of the buildings. One must make sure that the residual values

Table 12.4 Project with a large property element

Investment:	£
Plant and machinery	60,000
Land and buildings	100,000
	160,000
Annual cash flows:	
£9,000 p.a. (years 1–10) × 6.145	55,305
Residual value:	
Land and buildings: £300,000 × 0.350	105,000
Total present value	160,305

in such cases are based upon money units of present purchasing power, or perhaps more positively, to look at the investment in land buildings as a separate project.

Post-audit

As with any other technique based upon forecasting the future and making plans based on those forecasts, it is essential that the basic data used is of the highest quality. Even with sophisticated techniques like DCF, the end result of the appraisal process is only as good as the inputs of data that have been used. If these are poor, then no amount of calculation is going to make them any better.

To maintain and monitor the quality of the data used for this most important decision-making process, suitable methods should be evolved for checking the actual outcomes of projects that are approved against the original data. An overall view of the success or failure of the process can be obtained by tracking the trend in the return on capital employed, since this, in a sense, is the aggregation of all past projects that are still in being. If a project relates to a unit of the business that has its own separate accounting and reporting system, e.g. where a new division is set up to market a new product, this will provide a simple way of checking an individual project. This is only likely to be the case in a few projects and other methods must be considered.

Checking back on forecasts is often disliked in industry, but if it is known that there will be no check on the actual outcome, human nature being what it is, there will be no pressure to ensure that forecasts are as realistic as possible. Only where it is known that the data used for project

162

selection will be tested against the actual outcome, and divergences investigated, will there be any real pressure to produce the highest quality of data. The checking and investigation process is also one where any mistakes that have been made can be used as a learning process to improve the quality of future information.

SUITABLE PROJECTS

The post-audit process will cost money and, like any other control tool used by management, the cost of the system must be weighed against its potential benefits. It is likely therefore that its use will be confined to the larger projects with variable inputs. If values are fixed by contract, then even large projects might need little or no monitoring. For the smaller projects it is probably sufficient to test a sample to assess the quality of the data.

For the larger project with variable inputs which might form a significant proportion of the operational activity of the business, steps should be taken, as far as possible, to record the results flowing from that investment decision separately. As a very minimum, the recording of the operating data for that activity should be arranged in such a way that the relevant data can be extracted if required. If sensitivity analysis has been used in the appraisal of the project it will have identified those elements in the project to which the rate of return is particularly sensitive, and it may be enough to monitor those factors and ignore those to which the rate of return is not sensitive.

RESPONSIBILITY

As far as possible the control of audit checks should not be the responsibility of staff who have been involved in gathering the original data. It is probably most appropriate to locate this function with the internal audit group, if one exists, who would normally report directly to top management. It might be useful to include for this purpose one or more members of the capital budgeting team so that lessons learned from the audit are fed back to those responsible for planning and approving capital projects.

TIMING

With smaller investment projects the post-audit check should take place fairly soon after the project is running, say twelve to eighteen months. The precise time depends on the complexity and timescale of the project itself, but should be as soon as possible after the project has settled down operationally. For those projects with long construction and commissioning periods, followed by a lengthy interval before the full operating capacity is used, the post-audit might start earlier. At defined stages of construction, commissioning, and build-up to capacity utilization, the actual events should be compared with the plan on which the appraisal was based, to see whether or not the original aims are being met.

COMPENSATING FOR MANAGERIAL BIAS

Different managers may have different attitudes to the appraisal process and there may be conscious or unconscious bias in preparing the data. Hopefully, the post-audit process will deal with any conscious bias that is used to secure approval for a project. The unconscious bias may occur because some managers are eternal optimists and others pessimists. If a record is kept through the post-audit process of the outcome of each manager's investment projects it might be possible to detect which managers are likely to provide pessimistic forecasts and which optimistic. It may then be possible to build into the appraisal system factors which would compensate for such bias.

Summary

At the beginning of this book emphasis was laid upon the need for managers to be more concerned with the profitability of the businesses that they manage. This was not emphasized so as to focus their attention solely to the rewards that this might bring to them personally. Individuals should rightly be concerned with their personal income, but the objective in increasing business profitability should go beyond such rewards. In the one-man business, profitability and personal return go hand in hand, since the profit earned by the business is reflected in the owner's wealth. In the larger business this direct link is broken. The individual's remuneration may well be linked with the prosperity of the part of the business that he manages, but the cause and effect between the two is not always seen to be so close.

In the large company, managed by directors with little ownership of the equity, that relationship becomes even more remote. The link between the providers of the risk capital and the management of the business that they finance is not close. Often management seems to consider itself to be, not the representative of the owners of the company, but a body that exists in its own right to run 'its' company, and to deal with their responsibilities to employees, the state, and to the community at large. All too often these responsibilities are taken to be more important than their responsibilities to the owners of the business. These attitudes derive, of course, not only from management's attitudes but also from the perceived indifference of shareholders as a whole.

It is right that management should bear in mind that the business does have responsibilities to people other than shareholders. The standing of the business in the community, its attitudes to environmental issues, etc., can have a real bearing upon its future success. The danger is that this division may obscure the relevance and importance of the profitability of the business. This danger is not only the narrow one that it may limit or reduce the return to the owners of the business, but there is the wider effect that it may have on the economy as a whole. In the long run the business that achieves a high level of profitability will be the one that is in the best position to improve the rewards to the people that it employs and provide the backing for future growth. The profitable firm is the one that is best positioned to reduce prices or give better value for money so promoting its own long-term welfare. The profitable business is the one that provides the resources through taxation necessary to the proper running of the state.

If, then, profitability is of the utmost importance to both business and the nation, it is right that managements should be judged by the profitability yardstick. Only then will they ensure that their decisions relating to investment within the businesses that they manage are based on sound principles. The profitability yardstick for that decision process is provided by DCF. It enables the rate of return to be estimated for each commitment of the firm's funds to specific uses, and to make some assessment of the risks and uncertainties that are almost certain to be inherent in the way the funds are used.

The measure of profitability of the business as a whole is the return it earns on the capital employed. Within individual businesses, capital employed is represented by the net assets that it owns, that mix of assets resulting from past investment decisions. Decisions that are being made now will in turn determine both the mix of future assets, both fixed and working capital, and the return that will be earned on them.

Investment appraisal is a key decision area, committing very often large sums of money for long periods of time. The quality of the decision-making process is one that can have long-term implications for the business and should be based upon both high quality data and the right appraisal method.

Appendices

Appendix A. *Present value of £1 receivable at the end of each period*

	Percentage									
Year	1	2	3	4	5	6	7	8	9	10
1	0·990	0·980	0·971	0·962	0·952	0·943	0·935	0·926	0·917	0·909
2	0·980	0·961	0·943	0·925	0·907	0·890	0·873	0·857	0·842	0·826
3	0·971	0·942	0·915	0·889	0·864	0·840	0·816	0·794	0·772	0·751
4	0·961	0·924	0·888	0·855	0·823	0·792	0·763	0·735	0·708	0·683
5	0·951	0·906	0·863	0·822	0·784	0·747	0·713	0·681	0·650	0·621
6	0·942	0·888	0·837	0·790	0·746	0·705	0·666	0·630	0·596	0·564
7	0·933	0·871	0·813	0·760	0·711	0·665	0·623	0·583	0·547	0·513
8	0·923	0·853	0·789	0·731	0·677	0·627	0·582	0·540	0·502	0·467
9	0·914	0·837	0·766	0·703	0·645	0·592	0·544	0·500	0·460	0·424
10	0·905	0·820	0·744	0·676	0·614	0·558	0·508	0·463	0·422	0·386
11	0·896	0·804	0·722	0·650	0·585	0·527	0·475	0·429	0·388	0·350
12	0·887	0·788	0·701	0·625	0·557	0·497	0·444	0·397	0·356	0·319
13	0·879	0·773	0·681	0·601	0·530	0·469	0·415	0·368	0·326	0·290
14	0·870	0·758	0·661	0·577	0·505	0·442	0·388	0·340	0·299	0·263
15	0·861	0·743	0·642	0·555	0·481	0·417	0·362	0·315	0·275	0·239
16	0·853	0·728	0·623	0·534	0·458	0·394	0·339	0·292	0·252	0·218
17	0·844	0·714	0·605	0·513	0·436	0·371	0·317	0·270	0·231	0·198
18	0·836	0·700	0·587	0·494	0·416	0·350	0·296	0·250	0·212	0·180
19	0·828	0·686	0·570	0·475	0·396	0·331	0·277	0·232	0·194	0·164
20	0·820	0·673	0·554	0·456	0·377	0·312	0·258	0·215	0·178	0·149
21	0·811	0·660	0·538	0·439	0·359	0·294	0·242	0·199	0·164	0·135
22	0·803	0·647	0·522	0·422	0·342	0·278	0·226	0·184	0·150	0·123
23	0·795	0·634	0·507	0·406	0·326	0·262	0·211	0·170	0·138	0·112
24	0·788	0·622	0·492	0·390	0·310	0·247	0·197	0·158	0·126	0·102
25	0·780	0·610	0·478	0·375	0·295	0·233	0·184	0·146	0·116	0·092
30	0·742	0·552	0·412	0·308	0·231	0·174	0·131	0·099	0·075	0·057
35	0·706	0·500	0·355	0·253	0·181	0·130	0·094	0·068	0·049	0·036
40	0·672	0·453	0·307	0·208	0·142	0·097	0·067	0·046	0·032	0·022

	Percentage									
Year	11	12	13	14	15	16	17	18	19	20
1	0·901	0·893	0·885	0·877	0·870	0·862	0·855	0·847	0·840	0·833
2	0·812	0·797	0·783	0·769	0·756	0·743	0·731	0·718	0·706	0·694
3	0·731	0·712	0·693	0·675	0·658	0·641	0·624	0·609	0·593	0·579
4	0·659	0·636	0·613	0·592	0·572	0·552	0·534	0·516	0·499	0·482
5	0·593	0·567	0·543	0·519	0·497	0·476	0·456	0·437	0·419	0·402
6	0·535	0·507	0·480	0·456	0·432	0·410	0·390	0·370	0·352	0·335
7	0·482	0·452	0·425	0·400	0·376	0·354	0·333	0·314	0·296	0·279
8	0·434	0·404	0·376	0·351	0·327	0·305	0·285	0·266	0·249	0·233
9	0·391	0·361	0·333	0·308	0·284	0·263	0·243	0·225	0·209	0·194
10	0·352	0·322	0·295	0·270	0·247	0·227	0·208	0·191	0·176	0·162
11	0·317	0·287	0·261	0·237	0·215	0·195	0·178	0·162	0·148	0·135
12	0·286	0·257	0·231	0·208	0·187	0·168	0·152	0·137	0·124	0·112
13	0·258	0·229	0·204	0·182	0·163	0·145	0·130	0·116	0·104	0·093
14	0·232	0·205	0·181	0·160	0·141	0·125	0·111	0·099	0·088	0·078
15	0·209	0·183	0·160	0·140	0·123	0·108	0·095	0·084	0·074	0·065
16	0·188	0·163	0·141	0·123	0·107	0·093	0·081	0·071	0·062	0·054
17	0·170	0·146	0·125	0·108	0·093	0·080	0·069	0·060	0·052	—
18	0·153	0·130	0·111	0·095	0·081	0·069	0·059	0·051	—	—
19	0·138	0·116	0·098	0·083	0·070	0·060	0·051	—	—	—
20	0·124	0·104	0·087	0·073	0·061	0·051	—	—	—	—
21	0·112	0·093	0·077	0·064	0·053	—	—	—	—	—
22	0·101	0·083	0·068	0·056	—	—	—	—	—	—
23	0·091	0·074	0·060	—	—	—	—	—	—	—
24	0·082	0·066	0·053	—	—	—	—	—	—	—
25	0·074	0·059	—	—	—	—	—	—	—	—

	Percentage									
Year	21	22	23	24	25	26	27	28	29	30
1	0·826	0·820	0·813	0·806	0·800	0·794	0·787	0·781	0·775	0·769
2	0·683	0·672	0·661	0·650	0·640	0·630	0·620	0·610	0·601	0·592
3	0·564	0·551	0·537	0·524	0·512	0·500	0·488	0·477	0·466	0·455
4	0·467	0·451	0·437	0·423	0·410	0·397	0·384	0·373	0·361	0·350
5	0·386	0·370	0·355	0·341	0·328	0·315	0·303	0·291	0·280	0·269
6	0·319	0·303	0·289	0·275	0·262	0·250	0·238	0·227	0·217	0·207
7	0·263	0·249	0·235	0·222	0·210	0·198	0·188	0·178	0·168	0·159
8	0·218	0·204	0·191	0·179	0·168	0·157	0·148	0·139	0·130	0·123
9	0·180	0·167	0·155	0·144	0·134	0·125	0·116	0·108	0·101	0·094
10	0·149	0·137	0·126	0·116	0·107	0·099	0·092	0·085	0·078	0·073
11	0·123	0·112	0·103	0·094	0·086	0·079	0·072	0·066	0·061	0·056
12	0·102	0·092	0·083	0·076	0·069	0·062	0·057	0·052	—	—
13	0·084	0·075	0·068	0·061	0·055	—	—	—	—	—
14	0·069	0·062	0·055	—	—	—	—	—	—	—
15	0·057	0·051	—	—	—	—	—	—	—	—

Appendix B. *Present value of £1 receivable annually at the end of each year*

	Percentage									
Year	1	2	3	4	5	6	7	8	9	10
1	0·990	0·980	0·971	0·962	0·952	0·943	0·935	0·926	0·917	0·909
2	1·970	1·942	1·913	1·886	1·859	1·833	1·808	1·783	1·759	1·736
3	2·941	2·884	2·829	2·775	2·723	2·673	2·624	2·577	2·531	2·487
4	3·902	3·808	3·717	3·630	3·546	3·465	3·387	3·312	3·240	3·170
5	4·853	4·713	4·580	4·452	4·329	4·212	4·100	3·993	3·890	3·791
6	5·795	5·601	5·417	5·242	5·076	4·917	4·767	4·623	4·486	4·355
7	6·728	6·472	6·230	6·002	5·786	5·582	5·389	5·206	5·033	4·868
8	7·652	7·325	7·020	6·733	6·463	6·210	5·971	5·747	5·535	5·335
9	8·566	8·162	7·786	7·435	7·108	6·802	6·515	6·247	5·995	5·759
10	9·471	8·983	8·530	8·111	7·722	7·360	7·024	6·710	6·418	6·145
11	10·368	9·787	9·253	8·760	8·306	7·887	7·499	7·139	6·805	6·495
12	11·255	10·575	9·954	9·385	8·863	8·384	7·943	7·536	7·161	6·814
13	12·134	11·348	10·635	9·986	9·394	8·853	8·358	7·904	7·487	7·103
14	13·004	12·106	11·296	10·563	9·899	9·295	8·745	8·244	7·786	7·367
15	13·865	12·849	11·938	11·118	10·380	9·712	9·108	8·559	8·061	7·606
16	14·718	13·578	12·561	11·652	10·838	10·106	9·447	8·851	8·313	7·824
17	15·562	14·292	13·166	12·166	11·274	10·477	9·763	9·122	8·544	8·022
18	16·398	14·992	13·754	12·659	11·690	10·828	10·059	9·372	8·756	8·201
19	17·226	15·678	14·324	13·134	12·085	11·158	10·336	9·604	8·950	8·365
20	18·046	16·351	14·877	13·590	12·462	11·470	10·594	9·818	9·129	8·514
21	18·857	17·011	15·415	14·029	12·821	11·764	10·836	10·017	9·292	8·649
22	19·660	17·658	15·937	14·451	13·163	12·042	11·061	10·201	9·442	8·772
23	20·456	18·292	16·444	14·857	13·489	12·303	11·272	10·371	9·580	8·883
24	21·243	18·914	16·936	15·247	13·799	12·550	11·469	10·529	9·707	8·985
25	22·023	19·523	17·413	15·622	14·094	12·783	11·654	10·675	9·823	9·077
30	25·808	22·396	19·600	17·292	15·372	13·765	12·409	11·258	10·274	9·427
35	29·409	24·999	21·487	18·665	16·374	14·498	12·948	11·655	10·567	9·644
40	32·835	27·355	23·115	19·793	17·159	15·046	13·332	11·925	10·757	9·779

	Percentage									
Year	11	12	13	14	15	16	17	18	19	20
1	0·901	0·893	0·885	0·877	0·870	0·862	0·855	0·847	0·840	0·833
2	1·713	1·690	1·668	1·647	1·626	1·605	1·585	1·566	1·546	1·528
3	2·444	2·402	2·361	2·322	2·283	2·246	2·210	2·174	2·140	2·106
4	3·102	3·037	2·974	2·914	2·855	2·798	2·743	2·690	2·639	2·589
5	3·696	3·605	3·517	3·433	3·352	3·274	3·199	3·127	3·058	2·991
6	4·231	4·111	3·998	3·889	3·784	3·685	3·589	3·498	3·410	3·326
7	4·712	4·564	4·423	4·288	4·160	4·039	3·922	3·812	3·706	3·605
8	5·146	4·968	4·799	4·639	4·487	4·344	4·207	4·078	3·954	3·837
9	5·537	5·328	5·132	4·946	4·772	4·607	4·451	4·303	4·163	4·031
10	5·889	5·650	5·426	5·216	5·019	4·833	4·659	4·494	4·339	4·192
11	6·207	5·938	5·687	5·453	5·234	5·029	4·836	4·656	4·486	4·327
12	6·492	6·194	5·918	5·660	5·421	5·197	4·988	4·793	4·610	4·439
13	6·650	6·424	6·122	5·842	5·583	5·342	5·118	4·910	4·715	4·533
14	6·982	6·628	6·302	6·002	5·724	5·468	5·229	5·008	4·802	4·611
15	7·191	6·811	6·462	6·142	5·847	5·575	5·324	5·092	4·876	4·675
16	7·379	6·974	6·604	6·265	5·954	5·669	5·405	5·162	4·938	4·730
17	7·549	7·120	6·729	6·373	6·047	5·749	5·475	5·222	4·990	4·775
18	7·702	7·250	6·840	6·467	6·128	5·818	5·534	5·273	5·033	4·812
19	7·839	7·366	6·938	6·550	6·198	5·877	5·584	5·316	5·070	4·844
20	7·963	7·469	7·025	6·623	6·259	5·929	5·628	5·353	5·101	4·870
21	8·075	7·562	7·102	6·687	6·312	5·973	5·665	5·384	5·127	4·891
22	8·176	7·645	7·170	6·743	6·359	6·011	5·696	5·410	5·149	4·909
23	8·266	7·718	7·230	6·792	6·399	6·044	5·723	5·432	5·167	4·925
24	8·348	7·784	7·283	6·835	6·434	6·073	5·746	5·451	5·182	4·937
25	8·422	7·843	7·330	6·873	6·464	6·097	5·766	5·467	5·195	4·948
30	8·694	8·055	7·496	7·003	6·566	6·177	5·829	5·517	5·235	4·979
35	8·855	8·175	7·586	7·070	6·617	6·215	5·858	5·539	5·251	4·992
40	8·951	8·244	7·634	7·105	6·642	6·234	5·871	5·548	5·258	4·997

Year	Percentage									
	21	22	23	24	25	26	27	28	29	30
1	0·826	0·820	0·813	0·806	0·800	0·794	0·787	0·781	0·775	0·769
2	1·509	1·492	1·474	1·457	1·440	1·424	1·407	1·392	1·376	1·361
3	2·074	2·042	2·011	1·981	1·952	1·923	·1896	1·868	1·842	1·816
4	2·540	2·494	2·448	2·404	2·362	2·320	2·280	2·241	2·203	2·166
5	2·926	2·864	2·803	2·745	2·689	2·635	2·583	2·532	2·483	2·436
6	3·245	3·167	3·092	3·020	2·951	2·885	2·821	2·759	2·700	2·643
7	3·508	3·416	3·327	3·242	3·161	3·083	3·009	2·937	2·868	2·802
8	3·726	3·619	3·518	3·421	3·329	3·241	3·156	3·076	2·999	2·925
9	3·905	3·786	3·673	3·566	3·463	3·366	3·273	3·184	3·100	3·019
10	4·054	3·923	3·799	3·682	3·571	3·465	3·364	3·269	3·178	3·092
11	4·177	4·035	3·902	3·776	3·656	3·544	3·437	3·335	3·239	3·147
12	4·278	4·127	3·985	3·851	3·725	3·606	3·493	3·387	3·286	3·190
13	4·362	4·203	4·053	3·912	3·780	3·656	3·538	3·427	3·322	3·223
14	4·432	4·265	4·108	3·962	3·824	3·695	3·573	3·459	3·351	3·249
15	4·489	4·315	4·153	4·001	3·859	3·726	3·601	3·483	3·373	3·268
16	4·536	4·357	4·189	4·033	3·887	3·751	3·623	3·503	3·390	3·283
17	4·576	4·391	4·219	4·059	3·910	3·771	3·640	3·518	3·403	3·295
18	4·608	4·419	4·243	4·080	3·928	3·786	3·654	3·529	3·413	3·304
19	4·635	4·442	4·263	4·097	3·942	3·799	3·664	3·539	3·421	3·311
20	4·657	4·460	4·279	4·110	3·954	3·808	3·673	3·546	3·427	3·316
21	4·675	4·476	4·292	4·121	3·963	3·816	3·679	3·551	3·432	3·320
22	4·690	4·488	4·302	4·130	3·970	3·822	3·684	3·556	3·436	3·323
23	4·703	4·499	4·311	4·137	3·976	3·827	3·689	3·559	3·438	3·325
24	4·713	4·507	4·318	4·143	3·981	3·831	3·692	3·562	3·441	3·327
25	4·721	4·514	4·323	4·147	3·985	3·834	3·694	3·564	3·442	3·329
30	4·746	4·534	4·339	4·160	3·995	3·842	3·701	3·569	3·447	3·332
35	4·756	4·541	4·345	4·164	3·998	3·845	3·703	3·571	3·448	3·333
40	4·760	4·544	4·347	4·166	3·999	3·846	3·703	3·571	3·448	3·333

171

Appendix C. *Depreciation and cash flow*

There are a number of misunderstandings about the relationship between depreciation and cash flow. It is included in the cash flows as defined in this book, but, at the same time, we say that there is no cash flow for depreciation since it is only a book entry. Others argue that depreciation does not determine cash flow on the grounds that if the basis for depreciation is changed it does not alter the amount of the cash flow.

To clear up this point, consider the following example. A company is set up to own and operate one machine. The balance sheet at the start of the enterprise is shown at *A*. All the trading periods are rolled up into one accounting period so that the machine is fully depreciated in that period. The profit and loss account for the period's trading is shown in *B*.

At the end of the accounting period the balance sheet would appear as shown in *C* (assuming that there are no debtors or creditors). The cash balance of £120 is derived from the difference between the cash income from sales and those expenses requiring a cash outlay.

A. Balance sheet at commencement

	£		£
Machine	100	Share capital	100

B. Profit and loss account for the trading period

		£
Sales		200
Less:		
	Expenses other than	
	depreciation	80
	Depreciation	100
Net profit		20

C. Closing balance sheet

	£		£
Machine	100	Share capital	100
Less Depreciation	100	Net profit	20
Cash	120		
	120		120

172

The *cash flow* is the difference between the cash inflow from sales and what we could call the 'cash' expenses. In *accounting terms* this cash flow is then divided into depreciation and profit. If, for example, it was now decided to spread the depreciation over two accounting periods rather than one, it would not affect the cash flow. All it would do is to divide the cash flow into different amounts for depreciation and profit. In the example they would change to £50 depreciation and £70 profit, with the cash flow remaining at £120.

Index